Battered, Broken, Healed

Also by Maggie Hartley

Battered, Broken, Healed

A MOTHER SEPARATED FROM HER DAUGHTER.
ONLY A PAINFUL TRUTH CAN BRING
THEM BACK TOGETHER.

MAGGIE HARTLEY

TRAPEZE

First published in 2018 by Trapeze,
an imprint of The Orion Publishing Group Ltd
Carmelite House, 50 Victoria Embankment,
London EC4Y 0DZ

An Hachette UK company

1 3 5 7 9 10 8 6 4 2

A CIP catalogue record for this book is
available from the British Library.

ISBN (Paperback): 978 1 4091 7702 9
ISBN (eBook): 978 1 4091 7703 6

Typeset by Born Group
Printed and bound by
CPI Group (UK) Ltd, Croydon, CR0 4YY

www.orionbooks.co.uk

Dedication

This book is dedicated to Jasmine, Hailey, Daisy, Polly and Louisa and all the children and teenagers who have passed through my home. It's been a privilege to have cared for you and to be able to share your stories. And to the children who live with me now. Thank you for your determination, strength and joy and for sharing your lives with me.

Contents

A Message from Maggie

I wanted to write this book to give people an honest account about what it's like to be a foster carer. To talk about some of the challenges that I face on a day-to-day basis and some of the children that I've helped.

My main concern throughout all this is to protect the children that have been in my care. For this reason all names and identifying details have been changed, including my own, and no locations have been included. But I can assure you that all my stories are based on real-life cases told from my own experiences.

Being a foster carer is a privilege and I couldn't imagine doing anything else. My house is never quiet but I wouldn't have it any other way. I hope perhaps my stories inspire other people to consider fostering, as new carers are always desperately needed.

Maggie Hartley

ONE

A Baby on the Way

In my opinion, there are few things in life more satisfying than the simple pleasure of a freshly brewed cup of tea and a Digestive biscuit. As I watched the plumes of steam rising from my mug and evaporating into the air, I sank back into the chair and sighed.

'Penny for them,' said my friend Vicky, her voice disturbing me from my daydream.

'What?' I asked, surprised. 'Sorry, I was miles away there.'

'I could tell,' she smiled.

'I was just thinking how nice it is to be drinking a hot cup of tea for once,' I told her.

'I know what you mean,' agreed Vicky. 'The amount of half-drunk cups of cold tea and coffee I find scattered around my house at the end of the day is ridiculous. But that's kids for you. There's never a spare minute.'

My friend Vicky was a foster carer at the same agency that I worked for. Every month they had a coffee morning for carers and their foster children. It was a nice opportunity for

1

me to catch up with other carers and for the children to all play together. Vicky had brought along the three children she was currently fostering – Janie, six, and four-year-old Teegan, who were sisters, and five-month-old Alfie. I was there with the four-year-old identical twin girls I'd been looking after for the last nine months, Daisy and Polly.

Eighteen-months-ago I'd made the decision to specialise in mother-and-baby placements and since then I'd had a couple of successful ones. But I was realistic, and knew there was a shortage of foster carers, so in between those placements I took on other children as well.

Fostering Daisy and Polly had been a challenge to say the least. Their mum was a heroin addict and they had been badly neglected. It broke my heart to see the horrendous state they were in when they were taken into care. They were like two wild animals that bit, scratched and lashed out. They were half starved and covered in flea bites and sores. Their long curly hair was so badly matted it had needed to be cut short. It looked brown when they first arrived but it was only after I'd treated the lice and washed it countless times that I realised it was actually blonde and it was just the months of grease and ingrained dirt that made it look darker. They had never been toilet trained and could only say a few words each. The one saving grace was that they'd had each other to cling to for comfort, but the poor little things had mostly been left to fend for themselves. It was unthinkable that a mother could let her children live like this. There was no denying that it had been a tough and intense few months for them and me, but after a lot of work and patience they had made brilliant progress. After months of therapy their speech and their play skills had come on in leaps and bounds. Their physical scars had healed but I knew they would carry the mental scars with them for life.

The girls had never had toys or been to a playgroup or a nursery, but they had learnt how to play and picked it up quickly and it was lovely to see them now sitting on the floor together playing while I took advantage of the peace and quiet. They might have been the mirror image of each other, but now their personalities were emerging I could see they were very different. Daisy was the bossier of the two while Polly was a lot more shy and quiet. Even though I wanted to encourage their individuality, I couldn't resist dressing them in identical outfits every now and again, and today they both had on the same grey jumper and unicorn leggings.

I didn't get many moments like this so I had to grab them when I could.

'How's Louisa?' Vicky asked.

'She's great,' I smiled. 'Still madly in love with Charlie. In fact she spends more time at his house than she does at home these days. I don't mind, though, as he's a lovely lad.'

'Ahh, bless,' sighed Vicky. 'I'm happy for her that she's got a nice boyfriend.'

Louisa had been with me since her parents had been killed in a car crash seven years ago. She was twenty now, so she was out of the care system, but she lived with me permanently. She'd been with me for so long, she was like my daughter. As a nanny, she was also a great help with my fostering placements.

'And while we're on the subject of boyfriends,' smirked Vicky, a mischievous look on her face. 'How's Graham?'

'Oh, give over,' I said, laughing. 'He's fine, thank you.'

After being resolutely single for years I'd recently started a relationship with an occupational therapist called Graham, whom my friend Anne had introduced me to on a rare evening out at her house. He was in his early forties like me, and I'd known him for a while before things had developed romantically.

'We're seeing each other but it's all very casual,' I told her. 'It's nice to have someone to chat to and to go out for a meal with from time to time . . . although since I've been fostering the twins there hasn't been much opportunity for that.'

'Hi Maggie,' said a voice suddenly, interrupting our conversation.

I looked over to see my supervising social worker Becky walking towards us.

'Sorry to interrupt but can I grab you for a quick word before you go?' she asked. 'There's something I want to run by you.'

'Of course,' I said. 'I'll pop into the office on my way out.'

'I think we can both hazard a guess at what that means,' said Vicky.

'Yep,' I smiled. 'No more hot cups of tea for me.'

We had both jumped to the same conclusion that Becky wanted to chat to me about a possible new placement. Curiosity got the better of me and there was no way I could wait to find out more. Vicky agreed to keep an eye on the twins so I gulped down my tea and went and had a word with Becky in the office next door.

Becky had been my supervising social worker for the past four years and we had a good relationship. She was enthusiastic and caring and she had two young children of her own so she had a good understanding of kids and their needs. I could always rely on her to fight my corner.

'Blimey, that was quick,' she said as I wandered over to her desk.

'Well, you know me,' I said. 'I'm itching to know what you wanted to chat to me about.'

'How are the twins?' she asked.

'They're doing well,' I said. 'The adoption team have started looking for parents for them and they start school next week.'

'Yes, I bumped into their social worker, Pat, the other day and she was amazed how far they've come since they've been with you. They look like different kids, Maggie.'

'We're still struggling a little bit with toilet training, but hopefully we'll get there before school,' I replied.

'That's great to hear,' she said. 'Anyway, while you're here I wanted to grab you to talk about a possible placement.'

'I'm all ears,' I smiled, intrigued to know more.

'It's not a mother and baby placement as such, but it is a baby,' she said. 'All I know is that it's a four-month-old girl. A child protection meeting happened this morning and Social Services are going to go to court this afternoon for an EPO. If the court agrees then I just wanted to check to see if you were in a position to take her?'

An EPO was an Emergency Protection Order that gave the local authority the right to remove a child who they felt was in immediate danger.

As with most of my fostering cases, I had to base my decision on whether to take a child on the least amount of information.

'I'd be happy to help,' I told her. 'You know how much I love babies.'

'Do you think you'll be OK coping with the twins and a young baby?' she asked.

'The twins will be at school full-time in a couple of weeks and then at some stage will hopefully be going for adoption, so I'm sure I can manage,' I replied. 'Besides, I'm ecstatic at the thought of having a house full of girls and I know Louisa will be too.'

The past few mother and baby placements I'd done had all been little boys, so I was excited at the thought of being able to indulge my love of pink for a change.

'Great,' said Becky. 'I'll let Social Services know that you're happy to take her on, and if you could be at home this afternoon just in case it all happens very quickly, that would be brilliant.'

'OK,' I said. 'Keep in touch.'

I went back to see Vicky.

'Well?' she asked.

'I think I've got a new placement on the way,' I said, grinning. 'In fact I'd better get home and start getting organised.'

Even though there were no guarantees the court would grant the EPO for the baby, they generally tended to listen to Social Service's concerns and I liked to be prepared.

I said goodbye to Vicky and managed to prise the twins away from the toys.

On the way home I called into the supermarket and bought some tins of formula and bottles and stocked up on several different sizes of nappies that I thought might work for a four-month-old.

I had two spare bedrooms that I used for fostering. The twins had the larger room that had bunk beds and a single bed in it. Luckily the smaller room already had a cot set up in it so all I needed to do was get out some baby clothes and toys I kept in the loft.

Becky rang later that afternoon as I was going through a pile of Babygros.

'Social Services have just phoned me,' she said. 'The court granted the EPO so they're going round to remove the baby now. They've asked the police to attend with them as apparently there are concerns there might be some trouble from Dad.'

'Oh, I hope not,' I said.

I hated to think of a little baby being caught in the middle of a violent scene. Taking a child away from its birth parents was always upsetting enough without the police having to be involved. Emotions were running high and it was never nice for anyone, especially the children themselves.

'Claire McDonald, the social worker, is going to take the baby to the hospital for a check-up first and then if all is OK, she'll bring her straight to you,' Becky continued. 'I've worked with her before and she's absolutely lovely.'

'No problem,' I said. 'I'll wait to hear more.'

It was always a strange feeling waiting for a new foster child to arrive. I carried on as normal, playing with the twins and getting them their tea, while my stomach bubbled with nervous anticipation. I kept glancing at my phone just in case I'd missed a call or a text.

There was still no news by the time Louisa got home from work just after 6 p.m. I was lurking in the hallway when I heard the click clack of her high-heeled boots on the front path. She towered over me these days and she was always so well dressed and groomed. She was a kind, caring soul, too, and I was so proud of the lovely young woman she'd become.

'What's wrong?' she asked. 'Are you expecting someone?'

'I'm waiting for a new placement to arrive and I'm a bit jittery,' I said. 'I don't know what time they're coming.'

When I told her about the baby, she squealed.

'Oh, I love babies, especially girls,' she said, her face lighting up. 'What's her name?'

'I don't know yet,' I told her. 'All I know is that she's four months old.'

'I can't wait to see her,' she continued.

But I still had no idea of when that would be. Just before 7 p.m. I took the twins upstairs to bed. I'd decided not to tell them about the new arrival yet until I knew more about her myself and I could answer their inevitable questions. It was a constant battle to get them both to have a bath, put their pyjamas on and brush their teeth each night, so it was a good 45 minutes before I had finished reading them a story. I was just coming down the stairs when I saw a shadow through the glass at the front door. I opened it before the short blonde woman on the doorstep had a chance to knock. A car seat was next to her on the floor but I couldn't see inside it as the hood was up.

'Good grief, you made me jump,' she gasped.

'Oh gosh, I'm sorry,' I said. 'You must be Claire, I'm Maggie. Come on in.'

She carried the car seat into the hallway and I peeped into it. The baby was fast asleep. She was a tiny little thing, looking more like a newborn than a four-month-old, and she had a head full of wispy golden hair. Her face was very gaunt and her skin was so milky white it was almost translucent.

'This is Jasmine,' she said. 'She nodded off in the car, bless her. It's been a long day for all of us.' She looked exhausted.

'Would you like a cup of tea?' I asked her.

'Oh, Maggie, you don't know how wonderful that would be,' she sighed gratefully. 'Today's been a bit of an ordeal.'

I warmed to Claire straight away. She was very bubbly and smiley and had a nice manner about her.

We went through to the kitchen and sat down. Louisa came to say hello and I introduced her to Claire.

'I wanted to see the baby,' Louisa said, glancing hopefully at the car seat.

'I'm afraid she's fast asleep at the minute, lovey,' I told her.

Claire took the hood down on the car seat.

'This is Jasmine,' she said.

'Oh, she's so cute and tiny,' gushed Louisa.

'Louisa's a nanny so she's very good with babies,' I told Claire.

'Well, aren't you lucky?' Claire replied. 'That's going to be very handy over the next few weeks.'

Louisa went upstairs to watch something on her iPad in her bedroom, leaving Claire and I to chat.

'So what can you tell me about Jasmine?' I asked her. 'Why was she removed from her parents?'

'To be honest, Maggie, I don't think even we know the full story yet,' she said.

She described how the family had been on Social Service's radar since Jasmine was born. A midwife in the hospital had expressed concerns because Jasmine's dad, Martin, had become aggressive with staff on the maternity ward when Hailey, Jasmine's mum, had to stay in hospital after the birth for a couple of nights because of an infection.

'Health visitors who called to see them at the house were often denied access,' she continued. 'Mum refused to let them in if Dad wasn't there. When they were allowed entry there were no squalid conditions. The house was very clean and very tidy, just very sparse and cold.'

Suddenly there was a noise from the car seat. Jasmine started wriggling around and flexing her back.

'Ah, someone's finally woken up,' said Claire.

She undid the straps and gently lifted her into her arms. Now I could see Jasmine properly I was struck again by what a tiny little thing she was and her neck was all floppy like a newborn. She stared up at me with her deep blue eyes as she adjusted to the bright lights of the kitchen, but they were devoid of any expression and she didn't make a sound.

'Dad had a good job in an office but he was recently made redundant so is at home all the time now. We suspect that he's very controlling. Mum is extremely quiet and it's possible she's depressed, although she won't talk to anyone about it. Our main area of concern was the baby, though.'

She explained that Jasmine had been classed as what the professionals called 'failure to thrive'.

'She's not putting on enough weight, although there were bottles at the house and plenty of formula. She's four months now but she's not rolling or babbling or holding her head up like she should be, and she's still in newborn clothes. The doctors can't find anything wrong with her and at this point in time we're just not sure what it is. But health visitors were concerned enough to call Social Services in.

'And you're just too little to tell us anything, aren't you?' she said, stroking Jasmine's cheek. 'A child protection meeting was held and there were enough concerns to get an EPO on the baby until we find out more about what's going on at home.'

'How did the parents react to the fact you were taking the baby?' I asked.

'As you can imagine, not great,' said Claire. 'We'd antici-pated problems with Dad so we arrived with the police in tow. He refused to let us in, so the police warned him we'd got an order to take the baby and that it was an offence to obstruct someone from removing the child if there was an EPO in place.

'When he finally let us in he was shouting and swearing and in the end the officers had to restrain him while I got Jasmine from her cot.'

'What about Mum?' I asked. 'How was she?'

'She didn't say a single word,' said Claire. 'But when she saw me walking out with Jasmine she dropped to her knees and started howling like a wounded animal.'

'Poor woman,' I sighed, my heart sinking.

'Neither parent was in any fit state to talk to us rationally so I left them my number. Hopefully I'll speak to them soon and explain what's going to happen and set up contact so they can see Jasmine.'

Jasmine started squirming on her knee and let out a low mewling cry.

'What time is she due a bottle?' I asked.

'Probably about now,' she replied. 'The hospital recommended putting her on a strict feeding routine to try and help build up her weight.

'Because she's so tiny, she'll need a bottle every three hours, even through the night.'

'Did she come with anything?' I asked.

'Nothing, I'm afraid,' said Claire. 'I wanted to get in and out of there as quickly as possible, so I took her out of her cot and put her straight in the car seat I'd brought.'

'That's no problem,' I told her. 'I've got plenty of stuff.'

'Is there anything else that you need before I go?' asked Claire. 'I will try and phone Mum and Dad tonight to let them know the baby's settled, but they might not be happy to hear from me.'

She stood up and carefully passed me Jasmine. For a four-month-old, she felt as light as a feather in my arms.

'I'll be in touch in the morning to see how things are going,' she continued. 'I hope you and Jasmine have a settled night.'

'I'm sure we'll be fine,' I replied.

I looked down at this tiny baby in my arms. She reminded me of a baby monkey as she stared up at me with huge blue eyes.

'Hello little one,' I cooed. 'Welcome to my house. I'm looking forward to getting to know you.'

TWO

First Days

Sitting in the rocking chair, I nestled Jasmine into the crook of my arm and got her comfy. I'd decided to bring her up to her bedroom to give her a bottle. It was after 8 p.m. now and even though she'd had a nap in the social worker's car, I was conscious that it was late and I should be trying to settle her down in the cot for the night.

One of my favourite things about caring for a baby was giving them a bottle. I loved how they gazed up at you with their big, trusting eyes as they gulped down the milk and how they felt all warm and snuggly in your lap. However, as I fed Jasmine her bottle she did none of those things. Her tiny body was so rigid and tense in my arms it was like I was holding a plastic doll.

'It's OK, sweetie,' I told her softly, hoping that the tone of my voice would help relax and reassure her. 'You're safe with me, don't you worry. Have some nice warm milk.'

Most babies were fascinated by human faces and would stare up at you, their gaze so unwavering it was almost unnerving at

13

times. But it was as though Jasmine was avoiding eye contact. Instead of looking up at me her eyes stared sideways at the wall or the ceiling. She occasionally took little glances but as soon as she caught my eye, she quickly looked away. I'd never seen a baby do that before and it was really odd.

'What's going through your little mind?' I sighed, stroking her cheek. 'What do you make of all this?'

If only she could talk and tell us exactly what had been going on at home.

Louisa came in and asked how I was getting on.

'She's OK,' I sighed. 'But she seems very tense and on edge.'

'Well, there's nothing wrong with her appetite,' she replied. 'It's a wonder she's so tiny. She's nearly finished that bottle.'

She was right. Jasmine had gulped down the lot in record speed. In fact, the powerful way she'd sucked on the teat and hungrily drunk it down reminded me of feeding a baby lamb.

As I held her on my knee and patted her back to wind her, I noticed how worn and tatty her Babygro was. It was covered in little patches of what looked like dried sick.

'I know it's late but I think I'm going to give her a quick bath,' I said.

Baths are good way of giving a baby a sense of routine and security, and it is always good to start as you meant to go on.

'Give me a shout if you need anything,' said Louisa, heading out of the door. 'I'm going to watch telly downstairs.'

'I'm sure I'll be fine,' I replied, laying Jasmine in the cot. I went to run a bath and got a nappy and clean Babygro out of the pile that I'd sorted from the loft. I knew the three- to six-month clothes would be way too big for her, but luckily I'd got a few zero- to three-month ones as well.

Before I put her in the water I stripped her down to her nappy.

I decided to change her on a mat on the floor rather than on the changing table. Babies her age tended to be very wriggly. They'd try and roll off the change mat or play with their feet and babble away, but Jasmine lay there as stiff as a little statue. As I undid the poppers on her Babygro I was struck by how pale and milky white her skin was, and without the bulk of her clothes she looked even more tiny and frail. There were no chubby cheeks or folds of flesh. She was scrawny and her skin was so transparent I could see the vivid blue and green of her veins beneath it. She was also covered in lots of dry, flaky patches and I made a mental note to give her a massage with some olive oil after her bath.

She didn't show any expression or reaction as I lowered her down into the warm water.

'Is that nice?' I cooed, splashing some water on her tummy. But she stared back at me blankly. She was such a quiet little thing.

After I'd washed her, I dried her off and quickly massaged some olive oil into her arms, legs and chest as well as a little bit onto her scalp where I'd noticed she had a few patches of cradle cap. Again she lay there stiff as a statue, not moving an inch. She was so compliant, I'd never seen a baby behave like this before.

I put on a clean nappy and Babygro and zipped her up into a sleeping bag. She seemed too tiny for the cot, so instead I decided she'd be cosier sleeping in the Moses basket that I had in the corner of the room.

'Night night, baby girl,' I said, laying her down and putting a calming hand on her chest to try and make her feel safe and secure.

She glanced at me with a blank expression and then looked away. One of the things I always did when I was putting young children to bed was to put on a CD of classical music. I found it helped relax and reassure them, especially babies, who preferred to have a bit of white noise rather than silence.

Most of the children I fostered had come from chaotic homes where there were often no bedtime routines or they didn't have a bedroom of their own to sleep in, so they found complete silence at night time unnerving and strange at first.

I also turned on a little night light so that it wasn't pitch black. I checked on the twins and went to the loo and by the time I'd been to the bathroom and come back, Jasmine was already fast asleep. The poor little mite had had a long day and she was obviously exhausted.

I went downstairs to sit with Louisa.

'Everything OK?' she asked.

'Yes, I think so,' I sighed. 'My heart always breaks for babies when they're taken into care. They're too little to tell us anything so we don't have a clue how they're feeling. It must be so strange for her not knowing where she is or who we are.'

'She's gone down OK, though,' said Louisa.

'She's probably shattered,' I replied.

As I went to bed that night, I couldn't stop the thoughts from whirring around my mind. What sort of a home had Jasmine come from? How had she been treated?

Apart from being dangerously underweight and floppy, Claire had said the doctor who checked her over at the hospital had found nothing medically wrong. Mercifully, she had no obvious injuries and there were no signs that she'd been hurt or physically abused. By all accounts the house she had lived in was clean and tidy and she had a proper cot to sleep in. Yes, her Babygro was a bit worn but compared to children like the twins who had suffered such horrendous neglect, this was nothing. But in the few hours I'd had Jasmine, I could tell from her demeanour that something wasn't right. Something had gone on in those four walls. I hoped we would eventually get to the bottom of exactly what it was.

I must have eventually nodded off, but halfway through the night I was woken up by a strange noise. It was a wailing sound and at first I thought it was one of my pet cats. It took me a few seconds to register that it was coming from the baby monitor.

Jasmine.

She had the quietest, strangest cry that I ever heard.

'I'm coming, sweetie,' I said, staggering groggily into her room where I saw she was lying wide awake in the Moses basket.

'What are you doing, missy?' I smiled. 'It's 3 a.m. and you're very alert. Were you wondering where you were?'

I picked up her stiff little body in my arms and I could see she was making sucking noises with her mouth and burying her head into my chest.

'You're hungry, aren't you?' I cooed.

I put her back into the Moses basket and quickly went downstairs and warmed up a bottle. She wolfed the whole lot down in a matter of minutes. After I'd winded her and changed her nappy, I sat down in the rocking chair and rocked back and forth hoping that it would help her settle.

Gradually, in the soft glow of the night light, I saw her eyelids flutter and eventually I felt her body soften and sink into me as she finally nodded off back to sleep. Gently I put her down in the Moses basket and crept back to bed.

I'd barely nodded off when the same thing happened an hour later. Her head was turning from side to side in the crib and she was sucking her fists.

'Are you hungry again?' I exclaimed.

I quickly went downstairs and warmed up another couple of ounces in a bottle. As before, she guzzled the whole lot down while I sat in the chair with her and rocked her back to sleep. By the time the twins woke me up at 6 a.m., I was exhausted and felt like I'd been up half the night. I took them downstairs and brought the baby monitor with me. Half an hour later I heard Jasmine stir.

'Now, I've got someone special that I'd like you two to meet,' I told Polly and Daisy. 'You wait here and I'll bring her down.'

The twins looked puzzled but their faces lit up when I walked back into the room with Jasmine in my arms.

'What's that?' Polly said when she saw her.

'I think you mean *who*'s that,' I smiled. 'This is baby Jasmine, and she's come to stay with us for a little while.'

Polly cooed over her, stroking her hair and trying to cuddle her a little bit too vigorously for my liking.

'You've got to be really gentle with little babies,' I explained. 'She's not a dolly so you can't pick her up. Maggie has to do it and we've got to be so careful not to squash her or fall on her.'

'I love the baby,' smiled Polly, but I noticed Daisy was very quiet.

'What's wrong, sweetie?' I asked her gently. 'Do you like babies?'

She shrugged.

'That's not our baby,' she sighed. 'Where's our baby gone?'

My heart sank. Daisy and Polly had a little brother called Ronnie but when the siblings were taken into care he was only six months old, so social workers had decided he would be a lot more adoptable on his own than if he stayed with his traumatised sisters. The harsh reality is that babies are in huge demand and are always easy to place. Placing older, more damaged children like Daisy and Polly, or a sibling group of three, is much more difficult. So Ronnie had been fostered by another carer and he had recently been adopted. The twins had asked about him a lot at first, but they hadn't mentioned him for a while. Seeing Jasmine had obviously brought it all back for Daisy.

'Remember what we talked about, Daisy?' I said gently. 'Your baby is going to have a new mummy and daddy, just like we're going to find you and Polly a new mummy and daddy too.'

'Is that baby getting a new mummy and daddy?' Polly asked, pointing at Jasmine.

'I don't know yet, sweetie,' I told her. 'She's going to live with us for a little while and then we'll see.'

I made the girls' breakfast and while they were eating their cereal, I gave Jasmine a bottle, which she again guzzled at speed. I was just getting everybody dressed when Claire rang.

'Hi Maggie,' she said. 'How are things this morning? How's Jasmine doing?'

'She's OK,' I said. 'She's eerily quiet for such a young baby. She even cries quietly, and it's more of a wail than a proper cry.'

'Yes,' said Claire. 'I noticed that yesterday.

'Has she been feeding OK?' she asked. 'I know that was the big concern at the hospital.'

'Absolutely fine,' I told her. 'She gulped down her bottle last night, she had two night feeds and one so far this morning, and I'm going to try her with another one in an hour or so. She seems really hungry, so I'll make sure I stick to feeding her every three hours.'

'That's great,' said Claire.

'What about her parents?' I asked. 'Have you heard from them yet?'

'Not a peep,' she replied. 'I tried Dad's mobile last night but there was no answer, so I left a message to say Jasmine had settled OK and left them my number. I'm going to try them again now. You'd think they'd be anxious to know how she is and to set up contact.'

'When do you think that will start?' I asked.

'I don't honestly know,' she replied. 'Because Dad's been a bit volatile in the past we'll have to hold it at the main Social Services building in town as there's plenty of security there. We'll need two contact workers to be in the room at the same time, so that might take a bit of organising.'

'OK,' I said. 'Keep me posted.'

As it was Jasmine's first day with me, we spent it quietly at home so I could get her into a good feeding routine. The twins had recently got into crafts so fortunately I was able to keep them busy with lots of sticking and gluing and making things out of Play-Doh.

Later that afternoon Claire called again.

'I've finally got hold of Jasmine's parents,' she said. 'Well, I spoke to Dad rather than Mum. They want to have contact

ASAP so I explained that it might take a couple of days to sort out, but in the meantime they've asked to meet you.'

'*Me*?' I said. 'How come?'

'Dad said they wanted to meet the person who was looking after their daughter,' she said. 'I know we don't normally do that but if you're OK with it I don't see why not. What do you think?'

'I think that should be fine,' I said. 'I suppose it's understandable. My only concern is that you've said Dad has been aggressive in the past so I'd be a bit worried he might turn on me or want to meet me to give me a mouthful.'

'We would warn him about that beforehand,' she said. 'I'd be there, as well as a couple of security staff. And you could bring your supervising social worker along for moral support if that would make you feel better?'

Normally, when there was an EPO in place, a social worker would come and pick the baby up and take her to contact. Or if I took her, a contact worker would meet me at reception to collect the baby from me and take it through to the parents. It was done that way because many parents, upset and angry that their child had been taken into care, understandably didn't want to see the person who was now looking after them. It was a way of avoiding conflict for everyone.

I knew I didn't have to say yes, but I also knew that if it was my child who had been taken into care I would want to meet the person looking after them.

I called Becky to get her opinion.

'You don't have to agree to meet them,' she said. 'But if you did want to then I'm happy to come with you.'

'Thank you,' I told her. 'I'd really appreciate that.'

I felt reassured and agreed to the meeting, which was arranged for the following day at the main Social Services building in town.

'I don't think it's a good idea to bring Jasmine with you as there's a risk that will inflame the situation,' said Claire. 'I've made it clear to them that this isn't a contact visit.'

'I completely agree,' I said. 'I'll ask my friend Vicky if she can take the twins and Jasmine for an hour or so while I come to the meeting.'

Vicky was happy to help out.

The following morning, I woke up feeling apprehensive. Jasmine had woken up twice for a feed so my head felt foggy from lack of sleep. I had to be at Social Services at 10 a.m. and it was a rush getting them all to Vicky's.

'Aw, what a sweet little thing,' she said when she saw Jasmine in her car seat. 'Isn't she tiny? She looks like a little dolly.'

'I know,' I replied. 'She's on a strict three-hourly feeding programme to try and build up her weight.

'I've just fed her but there are a couple of bottles in the change bag just in case.

'Oh, and watch the twins around her as they can be a bit over-zealous with their affection,' I added.

'I will,' she gave me a reassuring smile. 'Good luck with your meeting.'

I was intrigued to meet Jasmine's parents but I was also nervous. I just hoped they weren't going to give me a hard time.

I'd arranged to meet Becky in Social Services' reception so we could go in together and, to be honest, I was glad of the moral support. She asked me about Jasmine and I filled her in about how she was doing.

'Maggie, are you OK?' Becky asked, her brow furrowing. 'You're very quiet.'

'I'm a bit worried about how this meeting's going to go,' I sighed. 'For all I know Dad is using it as a way to have a go at me.'

'Well, Claire and I will be there and we won't put up with that sort of behaviour,' she said, putting her hand on my shoulder. 'If he goes off on one or is aggressive then it will be meeting over and Dad will be removed.'

I knew she was right, but as we got into the lift and Becky pressed the button for the fifth floor my stomach was churning with nerves.

'Honestly, it will be OK, Maggie,' Becky reassured me, sensing my unease. 'I'll be right next to you.'

But as the lift doors opened and we stepped out, I felt as if I was walking straight into the lion's den.

THREE

Meet the Parents

As we walked down the corridor, I saw Claire standing outside one of the meeting rooms. She waved at Becky and me.

'Hello ladies,' she smiled. 'We're in here. How's Jasmine today?'

'OK,' I replied. 'Still incredibly quiet but taking all of her bottles.'

'That's great,' she said. 'Feeding was everyone's main concern, so hopefully that means she's gaining weight. Anyway, let's have a chat later. Mum and Dad are already here so I'll take you in and introduce you.'

'How's Dad?' asked Becky. 'I heard he can be tricky.'

'A bit frosty,' she sighed. 'It's a bit like dealing with a moody teenager who doesn't like the fact he's not in control.'

Becky must have been able to tell I was on edge. She gave my arm a reassuring squeeze.

'It will be fine, Maggie,' she told me.

'Oh, don't worry,' added Claire. 'I'm confident that between the three of us we can handle him.'

I hoped she was right. I tried to ignore the fluttering of nerves in my stomach as I followed her into the meeting room where a couple were sitting around a large conference table.

'Maggie, this is Martin and Hailey, Jasmine's parents,' Claire told me, smiling reassuringly.

'And this is Maggie, the foster carer currently looking after Jasmine, and her link worker, Becky,' she told the couple.

'It's lovely to meet you both,' I told them, trying to sound as friendly as possible.

Martin scowled at me. Even though he was sitting down I could tell he was a tall, well-built man. He had fair hair that looked damp, as though he'd just got out of the shower. He gave me a curt nod.

'Hello,' mumbled Hailey, not making eye contact with me.

It was hard to even see her as she stared resolutely at the floor, her long dark hair like a curtain around her face.

As Becky and I sat down around the table, Martin frowned at me.

'Where's my daughter?' he said aggressively. 'I thought you'd be bringing her.'

'Another foster carer is looking after her,' I told him. 'She's very experienced, so I know Jasmine will be absolutely fine.'

'But why didn't you bring her with you?' he snapped, a scowl forming across his face. 'Why can't we see her?'

'Remember, I did explain to you on the phone yesterday that Jasmine wouldn't be coming today,' Claire told him, her voice calm and even. 'The purpose of this meeting was for you and Hailey to meet Maggie and ask her any questions. But we are keen to get contact started as soon as possible, so if you and Hailey have some time afterwards then we can have a chat and get the ball rolling.'

'I suppose that will have to do,' he huffed, clearly irritated.

'Would anyone like a tea or a coffee?' asked Claire breezily, doing her best to diffuse the tense atmosphere in the room.

'I'd love a tea please,' said Becky.

'I'll have coffee,' said Martin.

'Nothing for me thanks,' I told her.

'Hailey?' she asked.

She shook her bowed head, still not making eye contact with anyone.

While Becky made the drinks at the kettle in the corner of the room it gave me a chance to have a proper look at Jasmine's parents.

Martin looked like he was in his late forties and he was well presented in a crisp white shirt and a smart suit. Hailey, on the other hand, looked like she had just crawled out of bed. Her hair was greasy and unwashed and, although it was a warm day in early September, she was wearing a shapeless woolly jumper that was way too big for her. It had holes in it and what looked like bits of dried food down the front. She was very pale and thin with dark shadows under her eyes. I guessed she was in her twenties and a lot younger than Martin. They looked like such an unlikely couple and I never would have put them together.

Claire brought the drinks over. After a few sips of coffee Martin seemed to have calmed down.

'Before we start I just wanted to say I'm very sorry about the way I behaved the other day,' he told Claire. 'As I'm sure you'll appreciate, I was very upset and angry that my daughter was being taken into care. It was very frightening for us both seeing the police there and having strangers coming into our home and interrogating us. All we want to do is sort this mess out and get Jasmine back with us where she belongs.

'Isn't that right, Hailey?' He put his arm round his wife's shoulder and I saw her visibly flinch.

'Yes,' she murmured, looking up briefly, her eyes alert and fearful.

Her voice was so quiet it was almost a whisper.

I suppose after what I'd heard about Martin I had been expecting an aggressive yob but he seemed articulate and charming.

'Maggie, why don't you give Martin and Hailey an update about how Jasmine is,' suggested Claire.

'Is she smiling at you a lot?' he asked, leaning forwards. 'She's a very smiley baby.'

It was the complete opposite to my own experience of Jasmine so far, and I was surprised.

'She hasn't smiled at me yet, unfortunately, but she's only been with me a couple of days,' I said.

'Yeah, she doesn't know you from Adam, so that's probably why,' said Martin smugly. 'She only smiles at people she knows and trusts. She never stops smiling with us, does she, Hailey?'

Hailey nodded, her eyes fixed firmly on the floor.

'She's a very quiet baby,' I continued, 'but she's feeding really well, which is great.'

'Oh really?' interrupted Martin. 'She's normally difficult with her milk. Very fussy.'

'I haven't found that so far,' I said. 'In fact she's been happily taking a full bottle every three hours.'

An annoyed look flashed across his face.

'Well, how much are you feeding her?' he said. 'We don't want her getting fat.'

'Martin, do you remember how I told you that Jasmine had been seen at the hospital?' Claire cut in. 'For now, the doctors have recommended feeding her every three hours so we can get her to put on more weight. It's not a question of her getting fat, it's a question of her getting the food that she needs.'

'Well, whatever the doctors say I still think it's excessive,' he muttered.

I was astounded that anyone would be concerned about a four-month-old getting fat.

While he was talking, I noticed Hailey picking the skin around her fingernails. The nails were all bitten down and the skin around them was red and bleeding.

He was still firing questions at me when a contact worker came in to give Claire some paperwork. She was young and very pretty and Martin stopped what he was saying and looked her up and down.

'Oh, that's a lovely blouse, darling,' he said, flashing her a smile.

It made me cringe to see him trying to flirt with Social Services staff when we were discussing his baby being taken into care.

'What about night times?' he asked when the contact worker had left the room. 'Is she sleeping OK?'

'She's fine,' I said. 'She's woken up the past couple of nights for a bottle, but once she's had that she goes back down again no problem.'

'It's great news that she's settling and taking her milk so well,' said Claire.

But Martin looked disgruntled. He took a swig of coffee and then banged his cup down so heavily down on the table that Hailey jumped at the noise.

'Would it be possible for you to send some clothes for Jasmine?' I asked. 'It's nice when children have some of their own things around them, as they smell familiar.'

'Yes, we'll get that sorted,' said Martin. 'I'm sorry she didn't come with anything but it was all a bit of a rush and we'll do our best to rectify that. I'd really like her to be wearing her own clothes.'

'Hailey, is there anything you'd like to ask Maggie?' Claire asked her.

She had been incredibly quiet throughout the whole meeting and had hardly said a word. She looked at Martin almost as if she was asking for his permission to speak. She rooted around under her jumper and pulled something out of the pocket of her baggy jeans. It was a small, pink, slightly grubby-looking teddy.

'She likes to sleep with this,' she mumbled. 'It was mine when I was a baby.'

I noticed her hands were shaking as she passed it to me and as she caught my gaze for the first time I saw her blue eyes were filled with tears.

'Thank you,' I told her gently, my heart going out to her. 'I'll make sure she has it in her cot with her.'

She gave me a weak smile while tears streamed down her face.

I looked over at Martin, who had a face like thunder.

'Oh, Hailey, you never told me you were bringing that,' he snapped. 'I could have put it in with the other things.'

'I didn't want her to go another night without it,' said Hailey, trying to stifle a sob in her throat.

'Hailey, I don't think crying is going to help us,' he snarled. 'My wife gets very over emotional,' he said, turning to face us.

Hailey took a deep breath and wiped away her tears with the sleeve of her jumper in a bid to try and compose herself. I thought it was completely normal for Hailey to be so upset. I knew I'd be devastated if my baby had just been taken into care.

'I'm sorry that you're distressed,' Claire told her. 'I know you must be missing your little girl, which is why we want to make sure that you see her as soon as possible.'

'So are you bringing her to contact later today then?' Martin asked. 'We want to see her.'

'Unfortunately, it's not as simple as that,' said Claire. 'As I explained earlier, we'll talk about it after the meeting. Do you have any more questions for Maggie?'

'I don't at the minute, but if I think of anything can I ring you?' Martin asked. 'What's your phone number?'

I stiffened. For safety and confidentiality reasons, I very rarely gave birth parents my home number. Occasionally older children were allowed to have regular phone calls with their birth parents, but obviously that didn't apply to a baby like Jasmine.

'If you've got any questions, then you can ask me and I will pass them on to Maggie,' said Claire, cutting in.

'Also, when contact does start I always send a contact book along with the baby,' I explained. 'I write any important information in it such as how she's slept and fed or if she's been ill or if we've been out to a playgroup or anything.'

'Playgroup?' scoffed Martin. 'What a waste of time. She's just a baby. She can't even sit up, never mind play.'

'I find even the younger babies enjoy it,' I told him. 'They get a lot out of watching the older children and they have a little area especially for under-ones. You can also put any messages or questions in the contact book and I will get back to you.'

'Write them in a book?' he scoffed. 'I don't understand why I can't just ring you instead of faffing around with a book.'

'That's the way we do things and we normally find it works well,' said Claire. 'Hailey, do you want to ask Maggie anything else?'

Hailey shook her head and some fresh tears escaped from her eyes.

'I just miss her,' she sobbed.

'I know you do,' soothed Claire.

Hailey oozed vulnerability and I felt like reaching over the table and wrapping my arms around her, but I knew it wasn't appropriate. My overwhelming sense was that she needed looking after as much as Jasmine.

'Well, I think that's everything for now,' said Claire gently.

'Don't worry, Maggie and I will see ourselves out,' Becky told her. 'Then you can all stay and chat about contact.'

'That sounds like a plan,' said Claire. 'Maggie, I'll be in touch later.'

'Thanks,' I said. 'Nice to meet you both. I'm sure I'll see you again when I bring Jasmine for contact.'

'Maybe,' said Martin dismissively.

Hailey had stopped crying now and gave me a weak smile.

Becky and I walked out into the corridor and back towards the lifts.

'Thank God that's over,' I sighed. 'I can't put my finger on it but that man makes me feel really uncomfortable.'

He was very well presented and was obviously trying his best to be charming, but there was something about Martin that made my skin crawl and the hairs on the back of my neck stand up.

'Did you think it was a bit odd the way he looked at that young contact worker?' asked Becky.

'What, you mean the way he was undressing her with his eyes?' I replied. 'It was all very strange.'

'It's Mum that concerns me,' said Becky. 'She seems very anxious and jittery and she's so quiet. Dad comes across as very controlling and I think that needs to be investigated.'

I agreed.

As I drove to Vicky's, I replayed what had happened in my head. Meeting Jasmine's parents had given me a bit of insight into what her home life might have been. My gut feeling was that Martin liked to control everything. It would be interesting to see how they got on at contact and how they both parented together in front of other people.

I glanced at the grubby pink teddy poking out of the top of my bag. I could see how important that was to Hailey and that small act showed me that she was feeling a lot more than she was allowed to show. I was surprised how Martin had reacted when she had handed over that bear. I sensed that Hailey knew she'd upset him by doing something without his permission, and perhaps Martin was annoyed because he'd lost a tiny element of control.

'How did it go?' asked Vicky as I walked through her front door.

'It was all a bit strange,' I replied. 'Put it this way, there are lots of unanswered questions.'

I was deliberately being evasive and I knew Vicky didn't mind. Even though we'd been good friends for years, we didn't discuss our cases in detail as we both understood that we had to respect children's privacy.

'How have the twins been?' I asked.

'Fine,' she said. 'Although we've had a couple of pairs of wet pants, I'm afraid.'

'Ahh, the ongoing battle with potty training,' I sighed. 'I'm desperately trying to get it sorted before school next week. And what about Jasmine?'

'She's been as good as gold,' replied Vicky. 'She literally hasn't uttered a squeak. I'll put the kettle on. She's in the living room with Alfie.'

I walked in to find the twins watching TV and Jasmine lying on a play mat next to Alfie. He was only three weeks older than her, but the difference in size between the two of them was ridiculous.

'He's like a giant compared to her, isn't he?' laughed Vicky, walking back in.

It wasn't only their size that was striking; the two babies couldn't have been more different. Alfie was rolling around the floor, he had a rattle in one hand which he was sucking on and with the other hand he was batting the toys on the play gym and squawking at them. Jasmine was just lying there, as stiff as a statue, with a blank look on her face. Seeing them side by side made me even more painfully aware of how quiet and disinterested Jasmine was in the world around her.

Alfie had been removed from his mother at birth and Vicky

had looked after him since he was two days old. He was clearly thriving and was a happy, active, noisy little lad who was interested in everything, while Jasmine had switched off completely from the world around her.

'It makes me sad to see them together,' I sighed. 'Comparing her to Alfie really brings home how much more she should be doing.'

Alfie had been talked to, stimulated and nurtured ever since he'd been with Vicky. It was becoming obvious to me by now that Jasmine hadn't. When you think of neglect, people automatically think of a child being beaten, abused or starved. But mental and emotional neglect can have consequences as devastating as physical harm does. If a baby doesn't get the nurturing and stimulation it needs, it doesn't physically develop or reach its milestones.

I said goodbye to Vicky and took Jasmine and the girls home with a heavy heart.

Claire came round later that afternoon.

'I wanted to let you know that we've sorted out contact,' she said as we sat down at the kitchen table with a cup of tea. 'We decided on three times a week, at the main Social Services building where we were today, between 10 a.m. and midday. Dad wanted more but I explained that was probably enough for such a young baby.'

'When will it start?' I asked.

'In a couple of days, if that works for you,' she replied.

'That's fine,' I said. 'The twins start their settling-in sessions at school next week.' They were only doing half days at first. Having contact between 10 and midday would mean I still had time to drop them off and pick them up.

'You should have just rung me rather than feel you had to come round and tell me in person,' I told Claire. 'Not that it's not nice to see you, but I could have saved you a trip.'

'Actually, the reason I came round was to give you this,' she said, putting a Tesco carrier bag on the table.

'What is it?' I asked.

'Martin was adamant that Jasmine had her own clothes after the meeting earlier, so he brought this up to the office this afternoon and demanded that I take it straight to you. To be honest, the way he was talking about these clothes, I was expecting a suitcase filled with beautifully presented little outfits, not a supermarket carrier bag,' she said. 'But there you go. You have a look and see what you think.'

Intrigued, I peered inside the carrier bag and lifted the pile of clothes out. It was filled with tatty, worn and in some cases badly stained vests and Babygros.

'Why on earth is he insisting that I put Jasmine in these?' I sighed. 'Most of them look like they've seen better days.'

I always tried to listen to parents' wishes wherever possible, so I picked the four or five that were in the best condition and bunged them into the washing machine. It was puzzling that Jasmine's clothes were so worn as they didn't seem to be living on the breadline. He'd had a good office job when he was working and it sounded like they rented a nice house. His clothes were very smart when he'd come to the meeting at Social Services. So why was his child dressed in these rags?

'Just show willing, Maggie,' said Claire, seeing my dismay. 'Hopefully if Jasmine keeps putting on weight then she'll grow out of them soon.'

'I was going to go shopping anyway because she's so tiny and I'm short on nought to three-month clothes. I'll make sure to pick up a few extra bits for her,' I said. I got a small monthly clothing allowance for each child that I fostered.

'I haven't had the opportunity to buy baby clothes for a little girl in a while, but I'll try not to go overboard with the pink, I promise,' I smiled.

Claire laughed.

'While I'm here I also wanted to get your thoughts on today,' she asked. 'What do you think, now you've met Martin and Hailey?'

'I think there's a lot of things that need looking at,' I said. 'Martin was doing his best to be charming but he seems very controlling. Hailey is quiet; too quiet if you ask me, and that could perhaps be depression or anxiety.'

'I agree,' said Claire. 'The relationship between Mum and Dad definitely needs exploring and hopefully we'll know more soon, when contact starts.'

The purpose of having contact visits was not only for the birth parents to see their child, but for Social Services to see how they parented.

'I told Martin and Hailey that we've gone to the court for an interim care order,' she said.

An Emergency Protection Order lasted just 72 hours and it was only in the very rare case of a genuine misunderstanding that no further action followed. The majority of EPOs were turned into interim care orders.

'How did they react?' I asked.

'Even though I'd explained from the start that that was generally what happened, Dad was furious and Mum cried.

I also explained to them that that doesn't necessarily mean we'll go for a full care order. It's just a way of giving us more time to see them with their daughter.'

If Jasmine started putting on weight, if they found nothing amiss and if Hailey and Martin demonstrated that they would work with Social Services, then their daughter could go back home. But at this point in time too many things were setting off alarm bells – Jasmine's failure to thrive, Hailey's vulnerability, Martin's controlling attitude – and an interim care order was the next logical step. Failure to thrive is the term doctors use when a baby's weight gain slows down or halts altogether, or when they're not meeting their developmental milestones. Jasmine was a baby who had turned herself off from the world. The big question now was why.

FOUR

Small Steps

Some days nothing goes to plan. And today was definitely one of those days. It was such an important day – Polly and Daisy had their first half day at school and I was also taking Jasmine to her first contact session. I'd been so organised, laying out the girls' uniforms the night before and packing their school bags. I desperately wanted everything to run like clockwork but, despite my best intentions, my house was in a state of disarray.

I was still battling with toilet training the twins, so Polly was sat on the potty, Daisy was struggling to dress herself in her school uniform and I still needed to give Jasmine a bottle before we left.

'I'll stay and help you out,' said Louisa, seeing the chaos that was unfolding around her.

'But what about work?' I replied. 'You can't be late.'

Louisa was a nanny to a two-year-old boy.

'Liz works from home on a Wednesday so I'm sure she won't mind if I text her and say I'll be half an hour late.'

'Oh, I could kiss you,' I smiled. 'If you could do that, that would be wonderful.'

Louisa went to help the twins get dressed into their new uniforms while I warmed up a bottle for Jasmine.

'You're going to see your mummy and daddy today,' I told her as she gulped down her milk.

She still wouldn't meet my gaze for more than a few seconds at a time, but I always made sure I looked at her and talked to her to try and engage her.

'They're all ready,' said Louisa as the twins came trooping proudly into the kitchen wearing their new uniforms.

'Let me see you,' I said, my heart swelling with pride.

They looked so small and nervous standing side by side in their matching burgundy jumpers and pleated grey skirts and their shiny patent Mary Jane shoes. Their fluffy blonde hair was freshly washed and Louisa had brushed it and put a clip in Polly's and a black velvet headband on Daisy.

'Oh my goodness me, you two look so smart,' I smiled. 'You're going to have such a brilliant morning. There will be lots of exciting things for you to do and play with in your classroom, and Paris and Luke from playgroup with be there too.

'I'm just going to put Jasmine into her car seat and then we'll be ready to go.'

I was feeling a little apprehensive about how the twins were going to be on their first official day so I was trying to be as upbeat as possible. They'd had lots of settling-in sessions in their new classroom, they'd met their new teacher, Mrs Nevil, and they already knew some of the children from the playgroup that I took them to. But starting school was such a big step in a child's life, and particularly for children like

Polly and Daisy who had been through so much trauma and upheaval already.

'Have fun,' said Louisa as she waved us off before walking to the bus stop.

To my relief, both girls seemed chatty and excited in the car on the drive there. But as we pulled up at the school, they suddenly went quiet. Mrs Nevil was waiting outside the classroom door to meet them.

'In you go,' I said chirpily, giving them both a hug and a kiss on the head. 'Have a lovely morning and I'll be back to pick you up in a couple of hours.'

I could see Daisy was excited and she stormed off ahead. Polly, however, stopped and looked back at me anxiously.

'Go on, follow your sister, lovey,' I urged her. 'I'll see you soon.'

I need not have worried. Daisy, sensing her twin's nerves, ran back and grabbed her hand and the pair of them walked into the classroom together. Mrs Nevil came over to me.

'Don't worry,' she said. 'They'll be absolutely fine.'

'I know they will,' I sighed.

'And who's this?' she said, smiling at Jasmine in the car seat. 'You didn't have a baby with you the last time we saw you.'

'This is Jasmine, my new fostering placement,' I replied.

'What a sweet little thing,' she smiled. 'Anyway, instead of cooing over babies I'd better go in and see how my new class is getting on. See you later, Maggie, and honestly, don't worry.'

I knew I was so lucky to be able to send the twins to this school. It was small, caring and only a five-minute drive away in a nearby village. Many of my foster children had come to it over the years. I knew the teachers and the head well, and they'd always been really accommodating. Some of the staff had even had extra training about how to deal with 'looked after' children, as fostered or adopted children were referred to.

'Right, on to Social Services,' I said, looking down at Jasmine in the car seat.

I was pleased the twins' drop-off had gone smoothly. I could only hope Jasmine's did too. I was intrigued to see how this first contact session was going to go. I sensed that Hailey was genuinely desperate to see her daughter. It would be interesting to see how Martin reacted to Jasmine.

As Martin had behaved himself at the last meeting, Claire and I decided it was OK for me to take Jasmine up to the contact room myself. A new contact worker would be running the sessions, and I was keen to meet her and say hello.

I parked in Social Service's car park and when I went to get Jasmine out of the car I saw she was fast asleep. It was bad timing, but unfortunately there was nothing I could do about it. Babies often nodded off in the car and she was normally due a sleep around now. I knew she would wake up at some stage so her parents could have some proper time with her.

I signed in at reception and I got the lift up to the fifth floor. A young woman was waiting by the lift doors.

'Maggie?' she asked and I nodded.

'Hi, I'm Karen, the contact worker,' she said, shaking my hand. 'It's nice to meet you.'

I guessed she was in her twenties and she was casually dressed in jeans and a jumper.

She bent down to see Jasmine in her car seat.

'I'm really sorry, she nodded off in the car,' I said. 'But she normally only has half an hour in the mornings so she should be awake soon.'

'No problem,' she smiled. 'What's the saying – never wake a sleeping baby?

'Hailey and Martin are waiting outside the contact room,' she told me. 'Do you want me to take Jasmine down to them?'

'It's OK,' I said. 'I'll come down with you and say a very quick hello.'

It was important to be polite and I didn't want them to have seen me and be offended that I hadn't said anything to them.

As we walked down the corridor I saw Martin and Hailey sitting on plastic chairs. When Hailey saw me with the car seat, she jumped up and came towards us. It was then I noticed that she shuffled along rather than walked.

Her face was normally blank and emotionless but she broke out into a big smile and her eyes shone with tears as she saw her daughter. She crouched down on the floor next to the car seat and gently kissed the top of Jasmine's head.

'Hello baby,' she smiled, stroking her pale cheek. 'I've missed you so, so much.'

'I'm really sorry, she fell asleep in the car,' I said, taking off the blanket that was covering her as it felt quite warm in the building. 'I bet you're desperate for a cuddle.'

Hailey nodded. Her longing to hold her daughter in her arms was palpable.

'Aw, look at those cute dungarees,' beamed Karen. 'Doesn't she look lovely?'

I'd put her in the pair of flowery pink dungarees that I'd bought on a shopping trip the other day.

Martin's face was like thunder as he came over.

'Why isn't she wearing the clothes we provided?' he snapped. 'I specifically asked for her to be wearing her own things.'

'She's got one of your long-sleeved vests on underneath,' I said. 'I just bought her a few extras with the clothing allowance Social Services give me, as the weather's getting colder.'

'I only want my daughter dressed in my clothes from now on, not anything that you've bought her,' he snarled, squaring his broad shoulders.

'Enjoy your time with your daughter and I'll see you later,' I told them. I walked down the corridor and out to my car, feeling more uneasy with every step.

Rather than killing time in the town centre for the sake of it, I decided to head home and tackle some cleaning. I wanted to keep busy in a bid to try and stop myself from worrying. I couldn't stop thinking about both sets of children and how they were getting on. I hoped the twins were enjoying school and that Jasmine's contact sessions with her parents was going OK.

I wondered what the mood would be when I went to pick her up.

My house was gleaming by the time I needed to go back and pick up Jasmine. I drove back to Social Services and when I went up to the fifth floor Hailey was sitting on a chair being comforted by another contact worker.

'She got a bit teary having to say goodbye,' explained Karen.

Martin was waiting by the lifts, holding Jasmine in her car seat. She was fast asleep again.

'Do you want me to carry her out to your car for you?' he asked, all charm, his previous outburst forgotten. 'Where are you parked?'

'I'll be fine,' I replied.

'I honestly don't mind,' he insisted. 'I know how heavy this car seat is. I can put it in the car for you.'

'Martin, thank you for the offer, but I'm positive I can manage,' I said, holding out my hand to take the car seat off him.

My gut was telling me that I didn't want him to know what my car looked like. So I made an excuse about needing to check something with Claire while he and Hailey left the building.

When I walked into the office, Claire looked surprised.

'What are you still doing here, Maggie?' she asked.

'You'll probably think I'm mad but I wanted to kill some time while Martin and Hailey left,' I told her.

'Why, what happened?' she asked.

'Nothing in particular,' I said. 'I just got a funny feeling. Martin seemed desperate to know where my car was and where I was parked. I'm probably being over-cautious but I didn't want him to have that information.'

'No, you did the right thing,' she said. 'You have to trust your gut.'

'I can't put my finger on it but there's something about him that makes me feel uneasy,' I said.

At that moment, Karen walked in.

'Hi Maggie,' she said. 'I was hoping to have a word with you.'

'How did the contact session go?' I asked.

She shrugged.

'Odd is the only word I can use for it,' she said. 'Mum hardly said a word. Dad did all the talking.

'Unfortunately Jasmine slept for the first hour. When she did wake up, she was very disorientated and unsettled. I can't say she screamed or cried, she just made this strange wailing sound the entire time.'

'That *is* how she cries,' I said.

'The only time she was quiet was when Mum gave her a bottle, and then she went to sleep again,' she told me. 'Dad seemed very irritated by that.'

I looked down at her in the car seat, her eyes tightly closed. I wondered if she was so sleepy because she was coming down with something. Or it could have been her way of coping with the stresses and strains of what had happened to her over the past few days. It was early days and I knew from experience that it always took a while for everyone to settle into the routine of contact.

I glanced at the clock on the office wall and was suddenly filled with panic.

'Gosh, I'd better go,' I exclaimed. 'I've got to pick the twins up from school. I'll see you both in a couple of days.'

'Oh Maggie, before you go,' Karen called out after me, 'Martin wanted me to give you these.'

She handed me a carrier bag that had two grubby-looking dummies inside.

'Jasmine has a dummy?' I said, surprised as she had always settled perfectly well.

'Apparently so,' said Karen. 'I said I would pass them on to you so you could start using them.'

I slung the carrier bag on to the back seat of the car and soon forgot all about them on the drive to the school. My mind was whirring, wondering how the twins' first morning had gone. Jasmine was still fast asleep in the car seat as I dashed to the reception classroom.

'How did they get on?' I asked Mrs Nevil.

'They've had a great morning; they've done really well,' she replied, 'although Polly had a couple of accidents, I'm afraid.' She discreetly handed me a carrier bag.

'I'm trying really hard to crack the toilet training,' I sighed. Much to my relief, both girls came out smiling.

'How was school?' I asked them.

'It was good,' said Daisy.

'I did a wee in my pants,' Polly told me.

'I know sweetie,' I soothed. 'It doesn't matter. Shall we go home now and have some lunch?' They both nodded.

Jasmine was still fast asleep as we pulled up at home. She didn't wake up for another hour even when I transferred her from the car seat to her cot.

When she woke up, she seemed OK. It was hard to know how she was feeling as she was so blank most of the time, but even after all that sleep, she seemed absolutely exhausted. The twins were tired too and I was aware that all three of them had had emotionally draining mornings, so I made sure we had a very quiet afternoon at home. While Daisy and Polly had largely ignored Jasmine at first, they had now accepted her into our household and she was often included in their play. They would always bring her a toy and put it next to her in her bouncy chair, and they both wanted to help me when it was time to give her a bottle or change her nappy.

The next morning I dropped the twins off at school. This time both girls had a wobble as they couldn't believe they had to go again. It was starting to sink in that school was something that happened every day, which was a bit of a shock to them.

Just as I was walking back towards my car, my mobile rang. It was Graham.

'I've got an unexpected day off and I wondered if you fancied meeting for lunch?' he asked.

'I can't I'm afraid,' I said. 'I have to take my new placement Jasmine to see the health visitor.'

'I've hardly spoken to you since you got the baby,' he said. 'How's it going?'

'It's hard work, but she's a lovely little thing. Anyway,' I chided, 'you know I don't like talking about my fostering to you.'

Fostering is more than just a job for me, it's a vocation. It's something that's in my blood, and I live and breathe it. But that can feel overwhelming sometimes, so I actively seek out friendships with people like Graham who have nothing to do with my fostering. Because my home is also my workplace it's sometimes nice to go out and have a break, talk about something other than fostering and remember who I am again, rather than just Maggie the foster carer.

'Let me talk to Louisa and maybe we could go out one evening in a couple of weeks,' I suggested. 'I want to make sure the twins are happy in school and Jasmine is a bit more settled.'

'That would be lovely,' said Graham, his warm, soothing voice just the tonic I needed. 'I know you don't have much free time, but give me a shout whenever you're ready.'

'Thank you,' I said.

Fostering didn't leave me much time to have a social life.

I left school and drove straight to the GP's surgery for Jasmine's appointment with the health visitor. The hospital had advised regular weigh-ins and Jasmine had been with me for just over a week now, so I was anxious to see if she was putting on weight. If she wasn't, then I knew that tests would need to be done to check that she hadn't got a genetic problem or a medical condition that was causing her failure to thrive.

I knew Marie, one of the health visitors, really well. She'd done the job for even longer than I'd been fostering and I'd been to see her so many times over the years with lots of different children. She was a warm, friendly woman in her fifties with a kind nature and a lovely manner with babies and toddlers.

'Hello Maggie,' she grinned as I walked in. 'I haven't see you for a good few months. Who's this then?'

'This is Jasmine,' I said. 'I've brought her to be weighed.'

I explained about the concerns over Jasmine's failure to thrive.

'You strip her down to her nappy on the change mat over there and I'll pop her on the scales,' she said.

'How old is she?'

'Seventeen weeks,' I replied.

'What?' she gasped. 'Wow, she is a tiny little thing. I would have guessed she was only a couple of months, judging from the size of her.'

She expertly lifted Jasmine up from the mat and gently put her in the bucket part of the scales.

'Normally babies don't tend to like this bit because it feels cold on their skin,' she said.

But Jasmine didn't move or utter a single sound.

'Good girl,' she soothed as she wrote down the result on the chart the hospital had given me.

'She's a quiet little thing, isn't she?' she said. 'How long has she been with you?'

'Just over a week,' I said. 'I've had her on a strict routine of a bottle every three hours.'

'Well, it's obviously doing the trick, because she's put on just over a pound,' she replied.

Her weight was still very low for a baby of her age, but it was more than I had hoped for and a step in the right direction.

'That's brilliant,' I said. 'Her social worker is going to be very pleased.'

'Have you got her red book with you?' she asked.

When each child is born they are given a red NHS book for their weight and medical checks to be recorded in.

'I don't think we have it yet,' I said. 'I'll check with the social worker and she can ask the birth parents.'

'And is she up to date with her immunisations?'

'Again, that's something else I need to check,' I replied.

I walked out of the surgery with a smile on my face. It was only a pound but it was progress and it meant I was doing the right things. I got into the car and gave Claire a quick ring.

'I thought you'd like to know that I've just seen the health visitor and Jasmine has put on weight,' I told her. 'Just over a pound in the past week.'

'That's great news,' she said. 'Good work, Maggie.'

'It's nothing I've done,' I told her. 'I've just given her the bottles and she's drunk them.'

'At least we know there's probably no medical reason why she wasn't putting on weight,' she replied, 'although what it does do is raise more questions about her home life.'

I felt I was tackling the physical side of things, but it was the mental side that really concerned me and that wasn't such an easy thing to fix. Failure to thrive and develop was a complex issue when it involved more than just putting on weight. It took time and patience to help a baby like Jasmine become interested in life.

★

A couple of days later it was time to take Jasmine to contact again. After my unease around Martin at the last session, this time I'd arranged for Karen to come and pick the baby up from me in reception and drop her off again there too. I was always aware that sometimes when parents saw me it was a reminder that their child was in the care system and someone else was looking after them, and that could cause friction and animosity.

'Oh, by the way, Dad's written a note in the contact book for you,' Karen told me when I went to pick Jasmine up.

'I hope it's not about her clothes again,' I sighed. 'It pained me to dress her in that threadbare Babygro this morning, but I showed willing and I did it.'

I opened up the book and had a look.

Where is her dummy? He'd written. *She came without it!! I hope she's having it at your house like I requested.*

I showed Karen the note.

'Honestly, I've tried giving her the dummy several times over the past few days but she just spits it out,' I told her. 'In fact it made her cry. I'm not going to force a dummy on a baby who clearly doesn't want it.'

'Why don't you send it in with her for contact just to show willing, but don't use it at home if it's not needed,' she said.

I was always happy to do what I could to keep the peace and try and foster a good relationship with birth parents for the sake of their children. But my unease and distrust of Martin was showing no signs of abating. I'd only met him a couple of times but I could see it was all about control for him. He liked to be the one who called the shots at all times. My overwhelming feeling was that the dummy, like the clothes, was all about his needs. Who had Jasmine's interests at heart?

FIVE

Frustration

The next few weeks passed in a blur as we all got used to the new routine. The twins were exhausted from starting school and the time between pick-up and bed was hard work because they were both frazzled. But I couldn't complain too much – they had settled in well, much better than I could ever have hoped for, in fact. Like a lot of children who have suffered neglect, Polly was still struggling with toilet training and there was a plastic bag handed over to me most days when I came to collect the girls. Mrs Nevil had been really understanding about it and I knew that I just had to keep persevering and it would all click into place in time.

I told myself that perseverance was the key when it came to Jasmine, too. She had continued to put on weight but she was still worryingly quiet and stiff, and as the weeks had passed, I had begun to get more and more concerned about her.

Despite lots of stimulation, Jasmine is still very disengaged and disinterested in anything around her, I wrote in my daily recordings. These would be sent to my supervising social worker

Becky, as well as to Claire in order to keep them updated. *She shows very little response to anything, actively avoids eye contact and is still very silent.*

Going by my past experience, young babies tended to be resilient and most of them started responding after three or four weeks with me. But with Jasmine, we were five weeks down the line and I didn't feel like I was making any progress. It was hard not to feel deflated.

One morning I took her for her weekly weigh-in with the health visitor, Marie.

'She's doing brilliantly,' she smiled, looking at the scales. 'She's stacking the weight on now.

'Look at those lovely thighs. They're really chunking up.'

She was right, they were. It was really satisfying to see Jasmine's tiny, pale body begin to get more rounded. She wasn't chubby by any means, but she was beginning to get those bands around her wrists and her cheeks had slowly started to fill out.

'She's sleeping longer at night now, so do you think it's OK to drop her bottles down to every four or five hours?' I asked.

'Absolutely,' said Marie. 'She's coming up to 22 weeks so we should also be starting to think about weaning in another month or so. I wouldn't drop any of her bottles when you start the food, just try to get her interested and used to the textures.'

'You look worried, Maggie,' she said, as I got Jasmine dressed.

'Do I?' I sighed. 'I was just thinking how I wish the psychological side was as easy to sort as the physical. I'm trying everything, Marie, but I just can't seem to get through to her. I chatter to her all day, play with her; she watches the twins and is involved in everything we do in the house; but then I look in her eyes and there's nothing there. No reaction, no spark, no life. She's just blank.'

'Give it time, Maggie,' she told me. 'You're doing all the right things. You and I both know it will happen eventually and she'll start responding.'

But I honestly didn't know if she would. I'd never fostered a baby who had such a complete lack of engagement before.

'Thank you, Marie,' I smiled. 'You're a very wise woman.'

'That's what I'm here for,' she smiled.

'Oh, before you go,' she added. 'Any progress on getting hold of Jasmine's red book or finding out if she's up to date with her jabs?'

'No,' I said. 'But you've reminded me to chase her social worker up about it. She was going to ask the parents for it.'

I walked out of the doctor's surgery trying not to feel despondent. Marie was right. All I could do was continue to do what I'd been doing – trying to make Jasmine feel safe and give her a sense of routine and continuity.

I had a supervision session already booked in with Becky the following day. That's where we chatted about how I was getting along with my placements and if I had any issues or concerns. I told her my worries about Jasmine.

'I feel like I'm banging my head against a brick wall,' I said. 'It takes such huge effort to even get the tiniest little bit of eye contact with her and even then it's literally for a few seconds.'

'Perhaps we need to start looking at the fact that there could be something else wrong,' said Becky. 'Something that's actually stopping her from responding and reaching her milestones.'

'Do you mean Global Development Delay?' I asked.

Becky nodded.

Global Development Delay was difficult to diagnose. Only time would tell but it was possible that Jasmine had some sort of learning difficulty and that was why she wasn't meeting her milestones and was so unresponsive.

'Maggie, it's also important to remember that it's early days,' she told me, her warm expression very reassuring. 'We still haven't got to the bottom of exactly what was going on at home and what, if anything, Jasmine has been subjected to.

'But it's clear to me that she's experienced some kind of trauma and you know as well as I do that it can affect babies in the womb before they're even born. To try and cure months of trauma in a few weeks just isn't possible. You've got to give it time.'

'I know,' I sighed, looking down at Jasmine, who was sat silently in my arms. 'I just find it really sad. She should be so curious about the world, wanting to move and explore and roll and make noise, but she just lies there in silence. That's not a life, that's just existence.'

I felt my eyes filling up with tears.

'Maggie, don't get upset,' said Becky, reaching across the desk to squeeze my hand.

'It just gets to me that such a young baby has already given up on life,' I told her, dabbing at my eyes with a tissue. 'She doesn't seem to get any joy from anything.'

I still had so many unanswered questions. What had led her to become like this? What had she experienced in her short little life?

'I know it's upsetting,' said Becky. 'But keep on trying and I'm sure things will start to change. We'll keep a close eye on Jasmine and keep updating your notes. Time will tell us whether we need to look at possible developmental issues.'

'Thanks, Becky,' I said. 'I don't normally let things get to me like this.'

When Becky had left it was time to pick the twins up from school.

Pull yourself together, Maggie, I told myself. I couldn't let the twins see me like this.

Life had to carry on with the hope that eventually Jasmine would want to be involved in it. When we got home after school the girls played dressing up while I sorted out some piles of washing. As I always did, I put Jasmine in her bouncy chair so she could watch them.

'Maggie, look,' laughed Daisy. 'The baby is a witch.'

I looked over at Jasmine to see the twins had plonked a witch's hat on her head.

'Oh, don't you look funny,' I said, going over to her. 'Are you going to put a spell on me, wicked witch?'

I took the hat off her head and put it on mine so she could see what it looked like.

'Does it suit me, Jasmine?' I asked, tickling her under the chin.

But she didn't react and turned her head and looked away.

'She never does a smile,' said Polly sadly. 'Why's the baby sad all the time?'

'She isn't sad,' I said, hoping my words were true. 'How could she be sad when she's got you two to play with? She just hasn't found her smile or her laugh yet. But hopefully we can teach her. And the more she watches you two play and have fun, the more she'll want to have fun too.'

'OK,' smiled Polly. 'We'll teach her.'

At this point Daisy, dressed as a fairy, was busy sweeping the floor with a toy broom. She suddenly let go of it and it dropped onto the laminate with a clatter. Jasmine practically jumped out of her skin. She threw her arms backwards and in the air, like babies do when they are startled, and she started to wail.

'Oh, sweetheart, it's OK,' I soothed, picking her up out of the bouncy chair. 'Did that noise frighten you?'

Her big blue eyes stared up at me. As I held her close to try and comfort her I realised that the only reaction she had ever shown me was fear. She would jump at the slightest noise – whether that was the toast popping up out of the toaster or the twins playing particularly boisterously. As I looked at her in my arms I realised that her anxiety reminded me of her mum Hailey. She was very jittery and anxious too. Perhaps Jasmine had picked this up from her?

All I could do was help Jasmine to feel safe and to keep trying to reach her. In my experience, the best way to stimulate a baby was by involving her in normal life. I would hold her and talk to her as much as possible. When I was doing chores, I'd pull her bouncy chair around the house with me and chat to her while I was cleaning. When I was putting the dirty clothes into the washing machine I'd sit her in the washing basket. Wherever I went in the house, I took her with me in the hope that she'd watch and start to take an interest in what I was doing.

'Are you helping me, Jasmine?' I'd ask. 'You're being very useful.'

She was physically very stiff, too, so I wanted to try and get her to loosen up. I'd sit her on my lap and make a cycling motion with her legs to try and get her used to the feeling of them moving and encourage her to try and do it herself.

I went round to Vicky's house one day as I thought it would be good for Jasmine to spend some time with Alfie. He was nearly seven months now and he was sitting up and a bundle of energy. Once again the difference between the two babies was staggering.

I lay Jasmine under Alfie's old play arch and pushed the brightly coloured animals so they swung back and forth in the hope she might reach out for them.

'Look, Jasmine,' I said. 'Can you see the cow? It squeaks when you squeeze it.'

But Jasmine just lay there, as silent and still as ever. She didn't even show any reaction when Alfie leaned over and pulled one of the socks off her feet, before having a good suck on it.

'She's still such a quiet little thing,' sighed Vicky as we watched them both.

'She is,' I replied. 'But I'm trying to be hopeful that that will start to change.'

Jasmine was nowhere near sitting up yet but I knew I needed to encourage the muscles in her body to work so that she'd be strong and supple enough to do it eventually. I'd been sitting her between my legs on the floor, but that afternoon when I got home from Vicky's I thought I'd try her in a high chair. It looked so comical I couldn't help but laugh. This baby, the size of a two-month-old, looked even tinier strapped into a big padded chair.

Jasmine wasn't grasping or holding things in her hands yet, so I filled the tray on the high chair with spinners and toys that lit up or made a noise. I put a rattle in her palm and got her fingers to curl around it then I moved her arm up and down so she could hear that it jingled. I hoped that would get her interest and she would want to hold it and shake it herself. But as soon as I let go, her hand opened and the rattle dropped to the floor. She sat there, staring into space.

I did 'Round and Round the Garden' on her palm and sang her songs. We played peekaboo with a crocheted blanket so she had the reassurance of seeing me through the holes. I did it at first and then tried it on her.

'Where's Jasmine?' I said, lifting up the blanket. 'Peekaboo.'

But again, there was nothing. She stared back at me blankly.

Her face lacked any kind of expression and the only way I could try and teach her that was to over-exaggerate mine. Babies learn by copying, so I smiled a lot and did lots of silly voices so she could hear my voice changing. We went back to basics and I stuck my tongue out at her, like I do with newborns, in the hope that she would eventually copy me.

'Where's your tongue, Jasmine?' I asked. 'Show me your tongue.'

I was in regular contact with Claire and we talked about the concerns we both had about Jasmine.

'The contact workers haven't been able to make observations about her because she's continued to sleep through most of the sessions,' she said.

'Still?' I asked.

'Yep, she only wakes to have a bottle, apparently, and then nods off again,' she told me. 'Obviously that's extremely frustrating for the birth parents and Dad especially is getting increasingly irritated.'

'I must say she's always incredibly sleepy when I pick her up,' I said. 'Then she'll sleep for another hour at home.

'The funny thing is on days she doesn't have contact she doesn't have a nap in the morning at all and seems fine.'

Unfortunately, there wasn't a lot we could do to stop a baby from sleeping.

'How is she at night?' asked Claire.

'She's brilliant,' I told her. 'She goes to sleep no problem at all and wakes up for one bottle. It's not like she's up and down all night.'

I tried getting her up earlier on contact days and giving her a nap at home before we left to drop the twins at school, but she wasn't interested.

'I don't know what else to try,' I told Claire. 'Even when she hasn't fallen asleep in the car on the way there, she's nodded off as soon as she's got to contact.'

'We'll just have to keep an eye on it and hope that it changes,' said Claire.

I also asked her whether there had been any update on getting hold of Jasmine's red book. 'The health visitor was asking whether she was up to date with her jabs but I couldn't tell her,' I said.

'I have asked,' replied Claire, 'but the birth parents have refused.'

'Refused?' I said, surprised. This was odd.

'Yep,' said Claire. 'Martin said the red book belonged to them and it was about their daughter, and they were keeping it as it was no business of ours.'

'I'll give it one more go and if he's still refusing to hand it over then we'll have to seek the court's advice.'

For all Martin's protestations about wanting the best for his daughter, his behaviour told a different story. Why wouldn't a father want to share basic information about her health with Social Services?

Mercifully, the issue resolved itself a few days later. When I went to pick Jasmine up from contact, Karen was waiting for me. Jasmine was fast asleep as usual.

'Has she been any more awake today?' I asked.

She shrugged, half-heartedly.

'She was awake for about 20 minutes,' she said.

At least that was a slight improvement.

'By the way, Maggie,' she said, 'Hailey asked me to give you this.'

She handed me a little red book: Jasmine's health records.

'What did Martin say about that?' I asked. 'I thought he was refusing to hand it over.'

'I don't think Martin even noticed,' said Karen. 'Hailey tucked it down the car seat just as she was leaving and whispered, "Give this to Maggie."'

When I got home, I had a flick through it. Worryingly, there was no record of Jasmine having had any immunisations. However, there were a few notes in there from the health visitor who had visited the family in the weeks after Jasmine's birth.

Mum very quiet and teary, I read. *Been denied entry the past two visits as Mum will only give us access when Dad is at home and he was out at the shops.*

Baby presenting as small although Dad wouldn't let us weigh her. Questions about bonding as no observations of Mum holding or interacting with the baby.

From reading that, it was clear there had been questions right from the beginning.

Jasmine had been with me for six weeks when Becky rang me one afternoon.

'I've just had a call from Claire,' she said. 'They're going to hold a review meeting next week.'

A review meeting was a chance for all the people involved in caring for a child, including the birth parents, to get together and discuss Social Services' plan for them.

'Social Services want to go to court and ask for a parenting assessment,' she said.

'I thought they might be leaning that way,' I replied. There were too many questions that hadn't been answered.

'They haven't got a full picture of their parenting at contact, partly because Jasmine spends most of it asleep. So they want to explore that more, as well as the relationship between Mum and Dad,' she continued. 'Dad is clearly very controlling and they feel they're all things that need to be looked at in more detail in an assessment.'

I agreed. Something was clearly going on there. Exactly what I couldn't put my finger on.

'Combine that with the fact that Jasmine has put on weight with you and is feeding fine, then it all suggests something wasn't right at home,' said Becky.

'Maggie, now this is happening that obviously means that this placement is going to go on for at least another three months while they carry out a parenting assessment. So I just wanted to check you're happy to keep Jasmine in the interim?'

'Absolutely,' I replied.

'I know the twins are likely to go for adoption in the next few months so you'll have that to deal with as well as the baby,' she said. 'Are you sure that's not too much?'

'It's honestly not a problem,' I told her. 'As you know, I've done adoptions in the past with other children in the house.'

'As long as you're sure, then I'll let Claire know ahead of the meeting next week.'

I didn't even need to think about it. There was no way I could give up on Jasmine now. It would be detrimental to move her to another carer. I'd been trying my best to make her feel secure, settled and relaxed. Any impact I'd had on her, however small, would be lost if she had to start afresh in a new home.

Besides, I so desperately wanted to help her. It broke my heart to see how disinterested she was. I wanted to see her thrive and learn to enjoy life. My work with Jasmine was only just beginning.

SIX

Decisions

As I closed the car door, I could see Vicky waving goodbye to me at the window with Jasmine in her arms.

'Good luck,' she mouthed and I raised my hand to say thanks.

If there was ever a day when I needed luck, it was today. I'd dropped Jasmine off at Vicky's as I was heading to Social Services for the review meeting. I felt uneasy about how it was going to go. From what I'd seen of Martin so far, he wasn't going to take kindly to the fact that Social Services wanted to assess his parenting.

The reality was that a parenting assessment would be incredibly intensive and invasive. It would cover a lot more than whether Martin and Hailey could look after Jasmine. It would explore their own childhoods, how they were brought up, how they met and responded to each other. I couldn't help but wonder how on earth Hailey would ever manage to get through such an assessment and cope with that level of scrutiny when I hadn't ever heard her utter more than a few words.

My mind was still whirring as I walked into Social Services, where Becky was waiting for me in reception.

'I don't know about you but I'm not looking forward to this,' I told her.

'It will be OK,' she said. 'Everyone has agreed this is the best course of action, so Dad will have to go along with it.

'The reviewing officer won't have time for any outbursts and if he kicks off, then he'll be asked to leave.'

I knew Becky was right, but it didn't stop me from feeling apprehensive as I walked into the meeting room. Claire and Marie, the health visitor, were already there as well as a man and a woman I didn't recognise. There was no sign of Martin and Hailey yet.

'Let me introduce you all,' said Claire. 'This is Neil, the independent reviewing officer.

'Neil, this is Maggie, the foster carer who's looking after Jasmine, and Maggie's link worker, Becky.'

'Nice to meet you,' I smiled, shaking his hand.

'Likewise,' he replied.

He looked like he was in his sixties and he had a grey beard and was wearing what looked like a hand-knitted jumper and cords.

The Independent Reviewing Officer, or the IRO, was the person who oversaw the case and represented Jasmine while she was in care. It was Neil's responsibility to check that everything that should be done for Jasmine was being done. An IRO was usually a social worker from Social Services but someone not directly involved in the case.

'And this is Helen, the contact manager,' Claire told us, turning to a friendly looking woman with red hair sitting next to her. 'She's here to give feedback on how the contact sessions have been going.'

Just as we'd finished our introductions, Hailey and Martin arrived. Martin strode in, a bolshy look on his face, wearing a shirt and tie, with his wife shuffling in meekly behind him. Again, Hailey was wearing the same tatty high-necked jumper and didn't make eye contact with anyone.

Martin nodded curtly to us all as he came in, but Hailey didn't say a word and kept her eyes down.

There was a spare seat next to me and Martin pulled it out. I assumed he was going to offer it to Hailey but he sat down abruptly on it. While Claire introduced them and got everyone a drink, Martin glared at me.

'So I see you've not brought our daughter yet again,' he huffed. 'Oh, wouldn't it be terrible if she saw us one extra time this week?'

'I was asked not to bring her to the meeting because she would get bored and restless and it might have been distracting for everyone,' I told him calmly.

No one else had heard what he had said to me and there was something about his manner that made me deeply uncomfortable. He seemed to deal with women in such an aggressive way and I was relieved when he got up and went off to the toilet.

It gave me a chance to speak to Hailey, who was sitting hunched over in her chair. Every time I saw her she looked so downcast. I couldn't even begin to imagine how hard it must be for her to be away from her baby. Now Martin was out of the way, I leant over to her.

'Jasmine loves sleeping with the teddy that you gave me,' I told her gently. 'I put it in her cot every night.'

She looked up at me gratefully and smiled, her sad eyes filling with tears.

I could tell that the teddy was terribly important to her and I wanted her to know that I'd listened to her and had done what she had asked me to.

'You really have got a beautiful daughter, you know,' I said.

Hailey nodded sadly as a tear spilled down her cheek.

'I miss her so much,' her voice cracked. 'I miss cuddling her at night.'

She looked so lost and desolate my heart went out to her. I leant over and gently touched her on the arm.

'Hopefully this will all be sorted out soon,' I told her. 'This meeting is about how we can move things forward.'

When everyone had got their drinks and Martin was back in his seat, Neil started off the meeting.

Martin seemed to like the fact that a man was in charge.

'What's all this about, mate?' he asked Neil, his voice so casual he could have been talking to an old pal. 'Why exactly are we having this meeting? Because if you ask me, it seems like a waste of time. It's time that we could be spending with our daughter instead.'

'I'm sure your social worker has explained to you,' replied Neil, 'that the purpose of a review is to look at where we are with Jasmine and to discuss what Social Services feel is an appropriate next step.'

'With all due respect, mate, an appropriate next step is for my daughter to come home with us where she belongs,' said Martin.

'Martin, it's crucial that you and Hailey listen to what's been said at this meeting, as we're going to be making important decisions about your daughter's future today,' Neil urged him.

'So are you going to be deciding what happens?' Martin asked.

'I listen to the information presented to me and then all of us will make a decision collectively about what we think is the best way forward for Jasmine.'

Martin sighed and shook his head.

It was Claire's turn to speak first and she explained how and when Jasmine had been taken into care.

'It was a police removal due to concerns about how the baby's father might react, and the baby was removed from the home quite quickly after the court granted an EPO.'

'Well, you have to understand I was very distressed about my daughter coming into the care system,' interrupted Martin. 'I wasn't going to just sit back and let somebody take my child.'

Claire carried on as though she hadn't heard Martin and explained the concerns around Jasmine's failure to thrive and the fact she hadn't put on weight.

'I've already told you she was very fussy about her milk and she had feeding problems,' Martin cut in.

'Martin, we're just letting everybody get up to speed on what's been happening,' Neil told him firmly, clearly tiring of his interruptions. 'There will be time for you to have your say.'

Next, Marie updated us all on how Jasmine had started to put on weight while she was in my care.

'Any issues with feeding?' asked Neil.

'None that I'm aware of,' she said. 'According to Maggie, Jasmine has been taking her bottles absolutely fine.'

'Well, she's obviously outgrown the issues she had when she was with us,' snapped Martin.

'My other concern is that we discovered recently that Jasmine hasn't had any of her immunisations,' she said.

'I've already told the social worker, I don't believe in jabs,' said Martin. 'We're her parents, so we should be the one who decides if she gets injected.'

'My main worry is that, given that Jasmine is a very frail and underweight baby, we wouldn't want to take the risk of her getting ill,' Marie continued.

'She's not having them,' he snarled. 'My daughter's not being injected with all sorts.'

'Well, if we can't come to an agreement, it's something we'll have to talk to the courts about,' said Neil.

Throughout all of this, Hailey hadn't said a word. She'd sat there chewing on her lip or picking at the scabbed skin around her nails.

Next it was the turn of Helen, the contact supervisor. She updated everyone about how the contact sessions had been going.

'Unfortunately, it's very difficult for me to give you much feedback on the contact sessions, as Jasmine has been asleep a lot of the time.'

'Yes, it's really not good enough,' said Martin. 'We hardly have any time with our daughter as it is and when we do, she's sleeping.'

'I appreciate that must be very frustrating for you both,' said Neil. 'Is there anything that can be changed that means the baby's more awake during contact?'

'I've tried everything,' I told him. 'I've tried giving her bottles at different times, giving her an earlier nap, not giving her a nap. But unfortunately there isn't a lot you can do to prevent a young baby from sleeping.'

'What about moving the time of contact?' he asked.

'We could try that,' I said. 'However, on the days she doesn't have contact she's actually awake at those times and is very alert. Even though she's slept at contact, she seems to come back exhausted and always sleeps a good hour after she gets back.'

'Absolute rubbish,' spat Martin under his breath.

I ignored him as it was my turn to address the meeting next. I talked about how Jasmine had been when she had first come to me.

'She's a lot more settled now compared to when she first came to me, and she feeds and sleeps well, but she's still desperately quiet for a little one,' I said. 'My main concern is that she has a complete lack of interest in life. She's still not reaching any of her milestones like rolling, grabbing or sitting up.'

'Well, that's because she's not at home,' interrupted Martin. 'She was doing that at home, wasn't she, Hailey? She was about to roll and she was always grabbing things, wasn't she?'

I couldn't believe what I was hearing. It was the total opposite to the little girl that I had been looking after, who barely moved and very rarely even made a sound. Hailey looked like a startled rabbit caught in the headlights after being put on the spot by her husband.

'Oh for God's sake, Hailey, open your mouth for once and tell them,' he snapped.

'Yes,' she mumbled, looking like she was about to burst into tears.

'Mr Henley, I must warn you that I'm not going to stand for aggression in this meeting,' Neil cut in, 'and if you speak to anyone like that, I will ask for you to be removed.'

'Sorry, mate,' he said. 'As I'm sure you'll appreciate I'm just devastated that this has happened. All I want is to get my daughter back.'

Neil finished his notes, put down his pen and turned towards Hailey and Martin.

'As you've heard,' Neil continued, 'Social Services still have significant enough concerns about Jasmine that they and I feel warrant further enquiries. So with that in mind, they're intending to apply to the courts to do a 12-week parenting assessment so they can explore things in more detail.

'Claire will go through things with you after this meeting but have you got any immediate questions about that?'

Hailey buried her head in her hands while Martin scowled and shook his head.

'This is ridiculous,' he exclaimed, thumping his fist on the table.

'There's absolutely no need for you to do a parenting assessment. My daughter has got over her problems with feeding. She just needed to get a bit bigger and now she's done that we need to bring her home with us.'

Hailey let out a gut-wrenching sob.

'I just want my baby back,' she wept.

I could feel her genuine pain and upset about her baby, and my heart went out to her.

The rest of the meeting was taken up with the practicalities of how and when the assessment would take place.

'We'll increase contact to four mornings a week,' Claire explained to them. 'You'll each come on your own one morning, and then you'll have two where you come together.'

Martin scoffed.

'I don't see why Hailey and I have to do separate sessions,' he said. 'Hailey doesn't like going out without me. 'Do you, Hailey?' His eyes bore down on her.

'I'll be all right,' she mumbled. 'If that's what I've got to do to get my baby back then I'll do it.'

I could tell by his face that Martin was annoyed that she was challenging him in front of a group of people. Hailey looked terrified, and sat there biting her nails, refusing to catch anyone's eye. It was the first time that I'd seen her stand up to her husband and it showed me how desperately she wanted her daughter back.

Claire explained that the sessions would now transfer to a family centre rather than being held at Social Services.

'It's much more comfortable,' she explained. 'It's set up like a flat so there's a kitchen where you can make food and drinks, and a living area with sofas and toys.'

'We're meeting later with the family centre to check the days are available. Until then we'll keep contact as it is now.'

Martin shook his head in disgust.

'Well, it looks like we have a plan of action moving forward,' said Neil. 'What I do need to add is that, given Jasmine's age, we really need to work out what is best for her future as soon as possible.

'If the parenting assessment doesn't work out for whatever reason, then plans need to be put in place to move quickly towards adoption.'

On hearing the word 'adoption', Hailey let out a huge cry, the sound of her pain echoing off the walls.

'Blubbing is not going to help,' Martin hissed.

Then he turned to Neil and gave a sinister smile.

'There's no way our daughter's going to go for adoption,' he said. 'Do this assessment if you wish and then hopefully you'll see that this has all been a terrible mistake.'

The meeting was quickly drawn to a close and I, for one, couldn't wait to get out of there. I could see Martin had tried to come across as charming but his aggressive interruptions, the way he spoke to Hailey and his unnerving stare made me feel ill at ease.

I nipped to the loo before I left but as I walked out of the building, my heart sank as I spotted Martin having a cigarette outside. I went the long way round to the car park so I didn't have to walk past him, and I was hoping that he hadn't noticed me. I drove back to Vicky's to collect Jasmine.

'How did that go?' she asked when I got back.

'Oh, you know,' I sighed. 'As well as it could have done when you're telling parents that they can't have their child back and they're going to be subject to more scrutiny.'

As necessary as a parenting assessment was, it didn't make matters any easier.

On the way back from Vicky's, I went and picked up the twins from school and we headed home. Polly and Daisy wanted to play with their dolls so I strapped Jasmine into her high chair where she could watch the twins while I got on with making dinner. As usual the girls got Jasmine involved in their play.

Polly put one of her dolls on the tray of the high chair.

'One for you, baby,' she told her.

'Are you playing too, Jasmine?' I told her.

She blinked back at me blankly.

I'd just nipped out of the back door to the bin when I heard a loud, ear-piercing shriek.

'Maggie, Maggie, come quick,' yelled Polly.

I ran back into the kitchen expecting the worst. Daisy was crying.

'What is it?' I gasped. 'Was that you shrieking, Daisy? What happened?'

'It wasn't me,' sobbed Daisy. 'I didn't do anything. It was her.'

'It was the baby,' said Polly, pointing at Jasmine. 'Daisy took the dolly off the high chair and the baby shouted.'

I went over to Jasmine.

'Oh my goodness,' I said. 'Was that you making that loud noise, madam?'

As if in response, she let out another angry screech.

'What is it?' I said. 'Are you cross Daisy took your dolly?'

I picked her up out of the high chair and gave her a cuddle. To be honest, I couldn't have been more delighted!

'Maggie, why are you smiling?' Polly asked. 'Jasmine was shouting. You don't like shouting.'

'I know,' I grinned. 'And usually I *don't* like shouting, but in this case it's OK because Jasmine is finally letting us know how she's feeling. She was telling you two that she was cross that you'd taken her dolly.'

'Sorry, Jasmine,' said Daisy, wiping her eyes and offering Jasmine the doll.

'Oh look, Jasmine, you've got dolly back,' I cooed.

I looked at her and stroked her cheek. 'Well, hello there, Jasmine. It's great to hear you telling us how you feel.'

After a long and stressful day, this was a little glimmer of hope that Jasmine was finally coming out of her shell. Had she really found her voice at last?

SEVEN

Mummy's Here

Jasmine shouting about the dolly might not seem like much, but to me it meant the world. For the first time in the two months that I'd been fostering her, I had hope. Hope that this stiff, unresponsive little baby was finally reacting and responding and that all my efforts to engage with her were actually getting through to her. It was also a relief to know that perhaps she didn't have any learning difficulties. I knew there were no quick fixes with babies who were failing to thrive, but over the next few weeks there were signs that Jasmine was slowly becoming interested in life.

One afternoon the twins were dancing around and singing their favourite songs. As usual Jasmine was propped up on my lap so that she could watch what was going on and feel involved.

'Twinkle twinkle little star,' sang Daisy, doing the actions. 'How I wonder what you are.'

Polly danced around next to her, joining in with the words.

'Up above the world so high, like a diamond in the sky.'

As their voices and laughter rang out, I looked down and saw Jasmine kick her legs. It was only for a split second and at first I thought I'd imagined it.

'Girls, sing that song again. I think Jasmine likes it,' I told them.

The twins didn't need any encouragement. As they jumped around the living room, Jasmine's skinny little legs kicked out in excitement. She had obviously surprised herself too because her little head turned around and her eyes sought mine as if to seek reassurance.

'Clever girl,' I told her. 'They're your legs. Were you having a good kick, sweetie?'

I bent down and moved them for her so she would recognise the feeling and, I hoped, understand that it was nothing to be fearful of.

It was just a couple of kicks but to me it felt like I'd won the lottery. I was bubbling over with excitement and I was desperate to share this little triumph with someone. Louisa was at work so I quickly picked up my mobile and called Vicky.

'You're probably going to think I'm mad for ringing you about this, but guess what?' I told her. 'Jasmine kicked her legs.

'The twins were singing a nursery rhyme and she kicked her legs in excitement. That's the first time I've seen her show a positive reaction to anything.'

'Maggie, you're not mad,' she laughed. 'That's brilliant news. I'm so pleased. I know how worried you've been.'

My only hope was that it wasn't a one-off and that somehow it would open the floodgates for Jasmine to start reacting. But although there were no more major breakthroughs over the next few days, I was sure that she was holding eye contact with me for a little bit longer than she had done before.

Be patient, Maggie, I told myself. That's all I could do. Jasmine would hopefully get there in her own time.

Now she was six months old, I'd started to try her with a little bit of finger food. So far she hadn't done much more than look at it, but I was determined to keep persevering. I was strapping her into the high chair one lunchtime when I felt a vice-like grip on my dangly earring.

'Ow,' I yelled. 'Jasmine!'

I managed to prise her fingers off it before she ripped it out of my earlobe. When I pulled away she gave me a furtive glace as if to say, *Yes, it was me*, and then quickly looked away.

Louisa came into the kitchen.

'What were you shouting about?' she asked.

'This little one decided that it was a good idea to try and yank out my earring,' I told her, rubbing my ear lobe.

'Oh no,' said Louisa. 'Did she hurt you?'

'Well, she did a bit, but to be honest I'm delighted as she's never grabbed anything before.'

'Oh yeah,' said Louisa, her face breaking out into a smile. 'You're right.'

I didn't mind one iota because it's what babies her age did. I'd learnt the hard way over the years that little ones loved grabbing a fistful of my long hair or pulling on my ponytail, so to avoid this I usually put it up in a bun. If I was fostering babies I also tended to stop wearing scarves around my neck, or necklaces or dangly earrings, because they were things little hands liked to grab. Up until now, I hadn't had to worry about any of that with Jasmine. I was so pleased that she was reaching for things that she was curious about.

Another day I put her on her play mat in the kitchen. I turned my back for a few minutes while I put something in the cupboard and when I turned round she wasn't on the mat. My heart momentarily stopped. But she was now lying several inches away on the hard laminate floor, looking stunned.

'Oh my goodness,' I cooed. 'You're such a clever girl. Did you roll over? Did that give you a shock? You certainly gave me a fright.'

My experience with babies who had failed to meet their milestones was that generally when they started to develop, everything happened at once. It was like a domino effect.

'Maggie, come quick,' Polly screamed one day, running into the kitchen. 'The baby's being naughty.'

'Naughty?' I said, rushing after her. 'What do you mean?'

'She was spitting at me and Daisy.'

When I dashed into the living room Jasmine was sitting in her bouncy chair looking very pleased with herself. She took one look at me, stuck her tongue out and reverberated it against her lips.

'See!' shrieked Polly. 'She's doing spitting at us.'

'She's not spitting, she's blowing raspberries,' I said. 'She's learning that she can make sounds with her lips.'

'Come on,' I said. 'Let's show her we can do it too.'

The twins thought it was hilarious as we all blew raspberries at each other. Jasmine kicked her legs in excitement and copied us.

It's like Jasmine's coming to life in front of my eyes, I wrote in my recordings that evening. *She's reacting to things around her and rolling, kicking and grabbing for things that look interesting.*

She wasn't laughing or smiling yet, but now I was hopeful that all that would come in time.

*

While all this was going on at home, Claire was busy making arrangements for Martin and Hailey's parenting assessment to start. The court had agreed to a full care order and also recommended that Jasmine should be immunised. She came round one afternoon to update me.

'Sorry I haven't been in touch for a few days,' she said. 'I'm trying to get everything set up for the assessment for Martin and Hailey, but I'm afraid there's an issue with the family centre.'

'What's the problem?' I asked.

'At the minute they can only offer us three sessions and as you know, we need four – two with both parents and one session for each of them individually.

'I've tried a few different centres but there's no availability in the local area, and I can't expect Martin and Hailey, or you and Jasmine for that matter, to travel too far that many times a week.

'So,' she paused. 'I was wondering how you would feel about one of the sessions being held at your house?'

I pondered the question for a moment before deciding I didn't have a problem with elements of that. However, I did have one concern – and it was a deal breaker.

'That's absolutely fine,' I said. 'I'm happy to help. The twins are at school in the day so I have the time. But I've got one hesitation.

'I'm really sorry, Claire, but I wouldn't feel comfortable doing a session with Martin at my house. To be honest with you, he intimidates me.'

'That's absolutely fine,' Claire replied. 'We don't want you to feel like that, so how about if Hailey comes and does her individual session here? That might be better suited for her, especially as she's so quiet,' Claire continued. 'She might feel more relaxed in a home environment than at the family centre. And out of all of us, she seems to have built up more of a rapport with you.'

She must have seen me talking to her at the review meeting.

'Yes, of course, that's not a problem,' I told her.

I was intrigued to spend time with Hailey on her own to see how she was when Martin wasn't around.

Years ago when I first started fostering, family centres weren't the norm so I regularly did sessions with birth parents at my house. Unfortunately, at one stage I had to do contact sessions with a man who had been to prison for serious, violent offences and I hated every minute of it. Nothing made me feel more vulnerable than having someone who I was uncomfortable with in my home, and I was terrified of this man. After four sessions I told the social worker I couldn't do it anymore and after that I vowed to be more cautious about the people I had coming into my house.

I was thankful Claire understood. Over a cup of tea, she told me how Hailey's sessions at my house would work.

'I'll get a contact worker to come here for a couple of hours so she can do some assessment work with Mum,' she said. 'Then you can cover the last hour where Hailey can just spend time with the baby.'

'That's not a problem,' I said.

'I'll pop in from time to time as I'd like to observe Hailey with the baby,' she said, 'starting with the first session next week.'

As part of the assessment work, Hailey would have to do basic tasks like preparing a bottle and giving it to Jasmine while the contact worker observed. She would also give Jasmine a bath and Hailey and the contact worker would talk about everything from first aid to the importance of play.

'With Hailey, I think we need to try and explore her relationship with Martin, as that's a specific area of concern for us,' Claire told me.

'Of course,' I said. 'We've all seen how aggressive he can be and she seems completely controlled by him.'

Now Claire had everything sorted, the sessions would start the following week. I felt like it was going to be a rocky road ahead as Martin and Hailey were put under the microscope. I wasn't sure how either of them were going to respond to the pressure.

The first session to take place was Hailey's at my house.

'I'll pop over, rather than the contact worker, for this first session just to say hello and to ease her into it,' Claire told me. 'She seems so fragile and so scared of everybody that I want to make sure that she's OK.'

Hailey was so painfully shy and quiet that I wondered what on earth I was going to say to her for three hours, but at least we would have Jasmine there as a distraction.

Social Services had organised a taxi to drop Hailey over at 9.30 a.m., when I would be back from taking the twins to school.

When I opened the door to her, she looked terrified.

'Hi Hailey,' I said. 'Come on in. Jasmine is in the kitchen on her play mat.'

She hesitated on the doorstep and seemed so unsure.

'Thanks,' she mumbled.

She was wearing a different polo neck jumper this time but it was still as worn and tatty as the other one. As Hailey shuffled into the hallway, I looked down at her feet and did a double take. She was wearing what looked like men's shoes. They were tatty black leather slip-ons and I could see they were several sizes too big for her, so it was no wonder that she shuffled. She must have seen me notice them because she stepped out of them and self-consciously pushed them under the radiator so they were out of sight.

'Here she is,' I said as we walked into the kitchen.

Hailey's face lit up when she saw Jasmine lying on her play mat.

'Would it be OK to hold her?' she asked hesitantly.

'Of course,' I said. 'She's your daughter. You can hold her whenever you want – you don't have to ask my permission.'

'Oh, thank you,' she said gratefully, breaking into a weak smile.

I watched her pick Jasmine up and hold her tightly in her arms. She closed her eyes and buried her nose in her daughter's sandy blonde hair, breathing in every bit of her.

'Oh my baby,' she murmured. 'I've missed you so, so much.'

I could see she was lost in her own world, savouring every moment of being with her daughter. Jasmine seemed calm and content in her arms.

Hailey stood, lingering by the sofa in the corner of the kitchen, looking as if she was afraid to sit on it.

'Relax and make yourself at home,' I told her.

She sat down and put Jasmine on her knee.

'She looks so pretty,' she sighed.

Happily, Jasmine was too big now to fit into any of the tatty Babygros that Martin had provided. Today I'd dressed her in a long-sleeved vest, cord pinafore and tights.

'I'm afraid I'm very old-fashioned in my tastes,' I told her. 'I love little girls in pinafores and pretty dresses with Peter Pan collars.'

'What sort of clothes do you like?' I asked as I poured the water out of the kettle into the teapot.

Hailey looked surprised. 'I don't know really,' she said, struggling to answer. 'Martin likes to choose Jasmine's clothes.'

I could tell she was incredibly tense and nervous. Her shoulders were all hunched and her hand shook as I passed her a cup of tea.

'It's OK, Hailey,' I reassured her. 'There's no need to be scared. We're all here to help you.'

'I know, but I have to get this assessment right for my daughter's sake,' she replied, her eyes almost pleading with me.

'I know you do,' I told her. 'But it's not about getting it right. It's about talking to you and understanding what things are like for you and Jasmine at home.'

We were interrupted by the sound of the doorbell and Hailey nearly jumped out of her skin. She seemed so on edge.

'That will probably be Claire,' I told her.

'What does she want?' she asked nervously. 'What will she ask me?'

'I think she just wanted to pop in and say hello as it's your first session,' I replied, trying my best to reassure her.

Claire came into the kitchen and I made her a cup of tea. She and I chattered away but Hailey hardly said a word. When

Claire did ask her anything, Hailey's voice was so quiet that Claire had to keep asking her to repeat things.

Watching her, I realised that Hailey's behaviour reminded me so much of Jasmine. She wouldn't make eye contact with anyone and when she did it was just for a few fleeting seconds. While Claire and I were talking she was constantly fidgeting, either picking the skin around her nails or pulling down the sleeves of her jumper. Even without Martin there she seemed jumpy and on edge.

When we'd all drunk our tea, I made my excuses and went upstairs to sort some washing, leaving Claire and Hailey to talk. A quarter of an hour later, Claire came out into the hallway.

'I'm going to get off now, Maggie,' she called up to me.

'How did that go?' I asked, coming down the stairs to let her out.

'To be honest it was hard to get more than a few words out of her,' she sighed. 'I don't know whether she's shy or it's just nerves or what. But it's going to be very difficult for a contact worker to do a proper assessment if she won't engage or open up.'

'It's her first session so she's bound to be nervous,' I replied. 'Let me talk to her. I'm sure she will be better next time.'

'I hope so,' sighed Claire.

I went back into the kitchen. Hailey was sat at the table picking her fingernails.

'How are you doing?' I asked.

Hailey shrugged. She looked so despondent.

'Did you find that hard?' I asked tentatively, sitting down next to her. 'Do you find it tricky talking to people?'

'Sometimes,' she said, avoiding my eyes. 'She was asking me questions and I didn't know what to say.'

'Just say what's in your head,' I told her. 'What kind of things did she ask?'

'Nothing about the baby. She wanted to know about Martin.'

'Well, it is an assessment about your whole family,' I said. 'And your marriage is an important part of that. She probably wanted to know if you're happy or if there's any conflict or disagreement and how you work through it.'

Hailey went really quiet. I could see her withdrawing into herself.

'I can't talk about it,' she mumbled, pulling at the sleeves of her jumper.

'Hailey, it's important to talk about it,' I urged her. 'Because this is about whether or not your daughter can come home.

'The whole reason you're having separate sessions to Martin is so that you have the freedom to say whatever you need to say. It doesn't mean everything's going to be repeated to your husband. It's just a way of talking through your issues.'

'I can't,' she sighed, hugging her arms across her chest. 'I don't think I can do it.'

I could see she was getting upset and I didn't want to push her any more. She seemed so vulnerable and I desperately wanted to try and help her. Because seeing her on her own with Jasmine had made me realise how much she truly loved her daughter.

'Let me show you around so you know where everything is for next time,' I said, in attempt to change the conversation.

I showed her all the rooms downstairs and then I took her upstairs to Jasmine's bedroom.

'What a lovely bedroom,' she exclaimed. 'There are so many nice things.'

She loved the Winnie-the-Pooh picture on the wall, and the blanket and the rocking chair.

'And look, she's got your pink teddy in her cot,' I told her.

'Thank you for doing that for me,' she said gratefully.

When we went back downstairs I asked her if she'd like to change Jasmine's nappy and feed her a bottle. Seeing her do these things perfectly, I was confused. Jasmine seemed content and Hailey talked to her and touched her. She knew how to interact with her daughter and I could see how much she loved and cared for her.

When the taxi arrived three hours later, I could tell she didn't want to leave Jasmine.

'I miss her so much,' she said, cuddling her tightly, breathing in her smell.

'You'll see her tomorrow at the family centre,' I said. But that thought didn't seem to bring her much comfort.

'I'll see you next week,' I said, trying to reassure her.

'Thank you for being so kind, Maggie,' she said.

After she'd gone I felt puzzled. From what I'd seen today, Hailey seemed a really capable mother. So why had Jasmine failed to thrive? Why was she so nervous and scared?

I phoned Claire to update her but she didn't answer, so I left a message.

'I've been thinking,' I said into the machine. 'Instead of the contact worker coming for the first part of Hailey's session maybe she could come for the last two hours. That would give Hailey time to relax and settle in before the worker came.'

I really felt for Hailey. I knew she was going to find this assessment hard and I wanted to try and make things a bit easier for her.

That night as I was putting Jasmine into her pyjamas, she grabbed for her vest and put it over her face.

'Are you playing games with me?' I smiled.

I pulled the vest off her face.

'Peekaboo!' I called.

She jumped a little bit but I tried it again.

'Peekaboo!' I repeated, and much to my amazement she gave me a little gummy grin.

Her first smile!

'You clever girl!' I grinned. 'What a gorgeous smile.'

I picked her up and did a little victory dance around her bedroom. My heart was bursting with pride as much as it would have been if she were my own daughter. It had taken her six and a half months but I was overjoyed that she finally felt safe and secure enough to smile.

Much to my surprise, I felt quite teary. I realised that these months of worrying that Jasmine had development delay, or that I wasn't doing my job properly, had taken their toll. These were tears of relief. All I could do now was encourage Jasmine to continue to express herself. It was the boost I needed. I wanted to look into her eyes and see life and excitement and happiness, not just blankness. Anything was better than the blankness.

But now I had to worry about her mummy, too. Things had started to change for Jasmine, but could I help Hailey? Before that could happen, I knew, she needed to open up to us. She needed to start telling us the truth.

EIGHT

Disappearing Act

After Hailey's session at my house, the next three days were going to be held at the family centre. To save me having to drive Jasmine there and back every day, one of the contact workers was going to come and collect her and bring her back to me. When she turned up I was pleasantly surprised to find that it was a lady I knew called Jan, who used to be a foster carer before she got the job at Social Services. She was in her fifties and was one of those people who you'd describe as the salt of the earth. She is a very kind lady and always smiling.

'Maggie!' she said. 'I haven't seen you for years. How are you?'

'I'm great, thanks. We'll have to have a proper catch up,' I said, as I handed Jasmine over to her in her car seat. 'Perhaps when you drop the baby off one day you can come in and have a cup of tea.'

'Yes I'd like that,' she replied warmly.

It is always nice to see a familiar face and deal with someone you know.

While she took the baby off I caught up on the pile of paperwork that I'd been neglecting over the past few weeks. Every so often I couldn't help but glance up at the clock on the kitchen wall and wonder how the assessment session was going. It was the first one at the family centre with both Martin and Hailey together.

Just over an hour after Jasmine had left, my mobile rang. When I heard Jan's voice on the other end of the line, I panicked.

'Is everything OK?' I asked, my heart pounding.

'Not really,' she said. 'Jasmine's been quite distressed, so I think we're going to cut today's session short. Is it all right if I drop her back to you now?'

'Yes, of course,' I said. 'Is she OK? What happened?'

'I'll explain more when I see you, Maggie,' she told me, sounding rather grim.

As I put the phone down, my mind was whirring as different scenarios ran through my head. What on earth could have happened to make Jasmine so upset? It didn't bode well that the first session had been cut short.

I was so concerned, I was already waiting at the front door when Jan pulled up outside. I couldn't hear any crying or wailing as she lifted the seat out of the car.

'How is she?' I asked.

'Fast asleep now,' she sighed. 'The poor little mite managed to get herself into such a state, but as soon as we left the family centre she nodded off.'

I showed Jan into the kitchen and then carried Jasmine upstairs and gently lifted her into her cot so she'd be more comfortable. She was in such a deep sleep she didn't even stir.

'What on earth happened?' I asked her when I came back down.

'She was just really unsettled,' sighed Jan. 'As soon as we got there she was very grizzly and as the session went on, she got more and more worked up and Dad couldn't seem to soothe her.'

'What about Mum?' I asked. 'She was very good with her when she was here yesterday.'

'Hailey wasn't there,' she shrugged.

'What do you mean?' I said, puzzled. 'Where was she?'

'Poorly, apparently,' said Jan. 'Dad phoned the social worker early this morning and said she was ill and wouldn't be coming to the sessions for the next few days.'

'Gosh, that surprises me,' I said. 'She seemed absolutely fine yesterday.'

Hailey had struck me as the kind of person who would drag herself out of bed to see her daughter even if she were on death's door. She knew how important this assessment was and it didn't look good not turning up. But I had to give her the benefit of the doubt. I'd seen for myself how much she loved her daughter, how much she missed her and how desperate she seemed to get her back. My gut told me that she would have turned up if she could.

'Hopefully she'll be back tomorrow,' I said, wishing it with all my heart.

'Martin didn't think so,' said Jan. 'He didn't think she'd be well enough for at least a couple of days.'

She was right. Hailey didn't turn up to the following day's session either. This time at least Jasmine was gone for the whole couple of hours. Again, when Jan dropped her back, she was fast asleep.

'How did it go today?' I asked. 'Was she any more settled?'
She shrugged.

'It's hard to tell,' she said. 'She was wailing and very fretful for the first half an hour, then she nodded off and slept for the rest of the time.'

'It's odd that she's so sleepy as she's dropped her morning nap now,' I replied.

'Maybe she caught something off Mum when she was here earlier in the week?' suggested Jan.

'Maybe,' I sighed.

It was all very strange.

'Did Martin say much about Hailey?' I asked, concerned. 'Do we know what's wrong with her?'

'Just that she had a nasty virus and was still very poorly.' said Jan. 'It's bad timing but what can we do? It's November and there are all sorts of bugs around.'

I thought she must be right.

Jasmine slept for another couple of hours after she left and when she woke up she was very clingy and wanted to be held all the time. But she didn't have a cold or a temperature and she wasn't being sick.

The same thing happened the following day. Again, Hailey didn't turn up for the final session of the week and Jasmine was still very unsettled.

'She wailed the entire time and by the end she had completely exhausted herself,' said Jan.

'What did Martin have to say about it?' I asked tentatively.

'He said that perhaps she was crying so much because of her digestive problems and implied that she was getting too much milk.'

'That's ridiculous,' I said. 'As far as I'm aware she doesn't have any digestive problems.'

By the end of the first four days of the parenting assessment, I was really concerned about Jasmine. She wasn't ill but it was as if she had regressed and gone back to the silent, stiff little baby that she had been when she'd first arrived. She had that frozen look, there were no more smiles, and the blankness in her eyes was back. Above all, she was just so, so quiet. Seeing her like this again made me realise just how far she'd come in the past few weeks. Since she'd learnt how to smile she'd been doing it constantly and she'd started making sounds like *oohs* and *aaahhs* and, of course, blowing raspberries. Now there was nothing.

At the end of the week, Claire phoned.

'How is everything?' she asked me. 'How's Jasmine doing?

'By all accounts, she's been very unsettled this week,' I replied. 'I think the new sessions have really taken their toll on her for some reason. She's exhausted, very clingy and incredibly quiet.'

'Do you think it could be separation anxiety?' she asked. 'It sometimes kicks in around this age. She could be getting upset because she's away from you – her main carer.'

'It could be,' I said. 'But she's normally fine being left. Vicky's had her a few times for me and she's never had a problem.

'How has Martin been with her?'

'He doesn't seem to be able to soothe her,' she replied, sounding dejected. 'In fact she gets more worked up when he picks her up. Hopefully Hailey will be back next week and Jasmine will settle into the new routine, but we will keep a close eye on it.'

If a baby was getting constantly distressed then it could be that the assessment process would be reviewed.

Over the next couple of days, to my relief, Jasmine seemed to gradually come back to life, and by the end of the weekend she was more active and making noises again. I hadn't heard anything more from Claire and I didn't know whether Hailey was going to be well enough to come to her session at my house.

But on Monday morning, just as I'd got back from dropping the twins at school, a taxi pulled up outside. Hailey looked very frail and fragile as she shuffled up the path.

'I'm sorry you've been so ill,' I told her. 'How are you feeling now?'

'Much better thanks,' she mumbled, staring at the floor.

She didn't look very well. There were dark shadows under her eyes and she looked pale and puffy. It was a cold day but she wasn't wearing a coat – just a scarf wrapped around her neck.

'Can I take your scarf for you?' I asked.

'Oh no, it's OK,' she replied quickly, worrying at the material of the scarf. 'I'll leave it on.'

She had a long baggy polo neck on and she kept pulling on the sleeves so they covered her hands. She didn't say much but I could tell she was pleased to see Jasmine. She picked her up and held on to her tightly.

'You look like you're enjoying that cuddle,' I smiled. 'You must have missed her when you were poorly.'

'I did,' she sighed, and I noticed the tears in her eyes.

I told her about the new arrangement that I'd discussed with Claire.

'From now on Jan the contact worker is going to come in the last part of our session,' I said. 'That way you can relax and get a bit of time with Jasmine first. I actually know Jan, and she's a lovely lady so you've got nothing to worry about.'

However, Hailey didn't seem very relaxed. In fact she seemed more nervous and on edge than ever. I could tell she didn't want to chat so I left her on her own with Jasmine.

When Jan arrived, I introduced them.

'Are you feeling better?' Jan asked. 'I heard you weren't very well last week.'

'Yes,' said Hailey uneasily, looking away.

I left them to talk in the living room while I went and made everyone a cup of tea.

'You must be boiling in that big scarf,' I heard Jan say. 'Do you want to take it off?'

'No, I'm fine,' Hailey replied firmly.

Hailey, made Jasmine a bottle and fed it to her. Afterwards she gave her a bath. As she checked the temperature I noticed the sleeves of her baggy jumper were trailing in the water.

'Hailey, love why don't you roll your sleeves up?' I said. 'They're getting soaked.'

'Oh,' she said, looking down. 'No, honestly, they're fine.'

As if to make a point she pulled down the sopping wet sleeves over her wrists.

The rest of the contact session passed without incident. After Hailey left Jan stayed for a quick chat.

'Blimey, she's a quiet one,' she said. 'Is she always like that?'

'She *is* quiet, but she was even more quiet than normal,' I replied.

'I didn't want to bombard her with too many questions today as she's been ill and she still seems a bit fragile.'

That was how Hailey was. She always had an air of vulnerability about her.

'But I can't fault how she is with her daughter, and Jasmine seemed very calm and content with her,' Jan continued. 'She knows what she's doing, she knows how to care for her and she was talking to her when she was giving her her bath.'

'She loves her,' I said. 'I can tell that.'

'Sadly, love isn't enough sometimes,' sighed Jan. 'Anyway let's hope the rest of the sessions go a bit better this week.'

Jan came to pick Jasmine up the next day to take her to the family centre.

'What are you up to today?' she asked me.

'I've got a morning of meetings,' I told her. 'The four-year-old twins that I'm fostering are about to go for adoption.'

Polly and Daisy's social worker was coming round to update me, along with an adoption worker. In a way, I was glad that my mind would be occupied so I wouldn't be thinking about Jasmine and wondering how the assessment session was going.

'It's non-stop, isn't it,' laughed Jan. 'I don't miss that about fostering.'

As soon as she left with Jasmine, the twins' social worker, Pat, arrived. She introduced me to their adoption worker, Helen, whom I hadn't met before. She'd just started working at Social Services after doing her training and, looking at her youthful face, she didn't seem much older than Louisa.

'How are the girls doing?' asked Helen.

'Brilliantly,' I said. 'They've been at school a couple of months now and they're really enjoying it.'

'Do you feel it's too soon to start the ball rolling with the adoption process?' she asked.

'I don't think so,' I said. 'They've settled in remarkably well and, touch wood, we seem to have cracked the toilet training in the daytime now.

'I've been talking about forever families to them and we've been reading lots of books about adoption to help prepare them.'

Helen explained that she had found a couple who were potentially a good match for Daisy and Polly and they were interested in finding out more about them.

'The good news is, they only live twenty minutes away from here so the twins can continue to go to the same school, which would mean less upheaval for them.'

That was good news indeed, and I was intrigued to find out a bit about the couple. After years of fertility treatment they'd finally given up on the idea of having their own biological children. The woman was a teaching assistant at a school and her husband was an accountant.

'They've got lots of extended family who live locally who can help,' said Helen. 'And they seem really excited and enthusiastic about the idea of taking on twins.'

'They sound brilliant,' I said, unable to keep the huge grin off my face.

'I'm hopefully going to meet them next week,' she told me. 'I'll tell them a bit more about the girls and I'll let you know what they think.'

It all sounded fantastic in theory but I knew in practice there were many hurdles ahead. The twins had been through so much and no matter how well they had done so far, I was worried about how they were going to cope with the upheaval of adoption. I knew I also had to get my head, and my heart, around the fact that they might be leaving me soon. I knew once the adopters said they were interested then everything moved pretty quickly. Within a couple of months they could be going in front of a panel who would decide whether to give them the go-ahead to adopt the girls.

But there wasn't much time to dwell on it. By the time Pat and Helen had left, Jan was due to drop Jasmine back. For once, the baby was wide awake.

'How did it go?' I asked nervously.

It was the first session that both Hailey and Martin had done together.

'It was fine,' Jan replied. 'Jasmine was still very grizzly and unsettled but she was a little bit better. She was definitely not as distressed as last week. What did stand out for me though was how different Hailey was today than how she is here.'

'What do you mean?' I asked.

'Well, when she was here she was quiet and not very chatty but she interacted well with Jasmine.

'Today she just sat there. I had to encourage her to pick Jasmine up, and she sat with her on her lap but she didn't talk to her, or play with her, or even cuddle her like she did here.

'She just seemed very stilted and robotic. And everything she did, she looked to Dad for approval.

'You can see she's completely under his control.'

'I think you've hit the nail on the head there, Jan,' I told her.

The more I saw, the more I was convinced. The root of all their problems lay with Martin.

NINE

Revelations and Accusations

Hailey sat on the sofa with Jasmine on her knee. It was her weekly session at my house, Jan had just gone and I could see how much Hailey was relishing being with her daughter without being watched or questioned.

'Ba-ba-ba,' said Jasmine. 'Da-da-da.'

'Oh, she's talking,' said Hailey, surprised.

'Yes she's making all sorts of noises now,' I smiled. 'She's really found her voice.

'In the mornings I hear her in her cot talking away to the teddy that you gave her.'

Jasmine was also grabbing at everything these days and suddenly she made a beeline for the thick scarf around Hailey's neck that she was still insisting on wearing. As Jasmine's tiny hands pulled at it, it came away from Hailey's neck and I glimpsed a mottled bright blue mark standing out against Hailey's pale skin.

'No, Jasmine,' said Hailey firmly, quickly adjusting the scarf back around her neck.

My heart raced. I was about to say something but I hesitated. Had I really seen what I thought I saw? Hailey had such transparent skin. Could it have been a vein rather than a bruise?

I was still mulling it over in my head as Hailey gave Jasmine a bottle. Afterwards, she put her on her play mat with some toys and went into the kitchen to wash her bottle up. As I went to take it off the draining board and dry it, Hailey pushed the sleeves of her jumper back and I saw a couple of raw, weeping burns on her arm.

I couldn't help but gasp in shock.

'Oh my goodness, Hailey! What happened to your arm?'

Hailey's cheeks burned red and she quickly pulled down the sleeves of her jumper.

'Nothing,' she snapped, looking down at the floor. 'I haven't done anything.'

'It doesn't look like nothing to me,' I replied. 'How did that happen?'

'Oh, I – er – burnt myself on the oven,' she said, biting the corner of her lip nervously. 'I'm really clumsy like that.'

I didn't for one second believe Hailey's excuse. I couldn't help but go into mother hen mode.

'They look really sore,' I said. 'You've got to be so careful with burns so that they don't become infected.

'Let me get my first aid kit and I'll clean them up and dress them for you.'

'No, no it's fine,' she said, backing away from me.

'Hailey, please let me help you,' I urged her.

She could see I wasn't going to take no for an answer, so she obediently sat down at the table. I brought Jasmine into the kitchen with us and put her in her high chair with some toys, then got my first aid kit out. I noticed Hailey wince as I pushed her sleeve up. It wasn't just one or two burns. Snaking all the way up the inside of one arm was a row of blistered spots. I wasn't born yesterday. I could tell from their shape and size that they were cigarette burns. I felt sick and angry with myself as I began to realise what Hailey was being subjected to.

'How did you say you did this again?' I asked, as I gently bathed them with tepid water.

'The oven,' she mumbled.

'Are you sure?' I asked as gently as I could. 'Hailey, you can tell me the truth you know.'

'I *am* sure,' she snapped, her eyes filling with tears. 'It was a silly accident.'

I could see she was upset and in pain so I didn't question her any more. I put some cream on them and bandaged her arm up to keep it clean. I knew that despite Hailey's insistence that it had been an accident, I would have to log what I'd seen in my notes as well as mention it to Claire.

'I've got to go now,' she said, pulling down her jumper sleeve. 'My taxi will be coming.'

She seemed relieved that we had run out of time so I couldn't question her further. She gave Jasmine a goodbye cuddle before we heard a car beep outside. I walked her out into the hallway.

'Look after yourself, Hailey,' I told her. 'I'll see you next week and make sure you change that bandage. I'll give you some spares.'

Hailey looked down at her arm and suddenly a panicked look flashed across her face.

'Oh no,' she gasped. 'I can't go home like this. I can't have a bandage on.'

Her hands were shaking as she frantically tore it off.

'Hailey, you need to keep that on to keep the dirt out of your burns and for them to heal properly,' I urged her.

'I can't, I can't,' she panicked. 'He'll notice.'

'Who will notice?' I asked her. 'Hailey, please tell me how you really got those burns.'

'I told you already, I burnt myself on the oven,' she snapped.

'What about the bruises on your neck?' I asked gently.

Hailey looked shocked and her hand instinctively went to her throat.

'I saw the marks when Jasmine pulled at your scarf earlier.'

I reached out and put my hand on her shoulder.

'Who did this to you, Hailey?' I asked gently. 'You need to tell me who has been hurting you.'

In my heart I already knew the answer but I needed to hear it from Hailey herself.

Hailey looked straight at me, her blue eyes filled with fear. She was like a rabbit caught in the headlights with nowhere to run anymore.

Tears spilled out of her eyes and ran down her cheeks.

'Martin,' she wept, her face in her hands. 'Martin did it. He burnt me and he tried to strangle me. He hurts me. He always has done.'

Then she fell to the floor in a crumpled heap. It was as though the burden of this terrible secret had finally consumed her.

My heart bled for her. I couldn't let her go home in this state. With Jasmine still in my arms, I quickly ran outside and told the taxi driver to go and then I led Hailey back into the living room. She collapsed onto the sofa.

I put Jasmine on her play mat on the floor so I could concentrate on Hailey, who was sobbing hysterically.

'You mustn't say anything,' she begged desperately, her eyes wild. 'Please don't say anything to anyone about this.

'Please, Maggie. He'll kill me. I know he will.' She was pale and trembling.

'Hailey, I'm so sorry but I have to,' I replied. I felt so awful, but I had no choice.

'I've got to tell Claire about this. People need to know. At the end of the day you've been hurt. You've been hurt by Martin, and Martin has contact with your baby. What if he hurts her too? It's my job to protect Jasmine and this isn't something I can keep a secret.'

Hailey looked over at Jasmine, who was rolling around on the floor, and started weeping again.

'You can't tell Claire because then I'll never get Jasmine back,' she wept. 'If Social Services find out what he's really like then she'll get adopted and I'll lose my daughter forever. And that would hurt me far more than Martin has ever done.

'I promise you he's never ever hurt Jasmine. If he did, I'd kill him. He's never touched her,' she sobbed, wiping her nose on her tattered sleeve. 'It's just me, Maggie, I swear. She's safe. She's absolutely fine.'

I could see how desperate Hailey was. I knew it was harsh, but I needed to make her see the reality of the situation.

'Hailey, I know you would never let him touch Jasmine or hurt her but he *is* hurting her by the way he treats you.

'Even though she's only a baby, Jasmine can sense what's going on. Every time you feel scared and frightened, she feels that too. Every time there's screaming or shouting or crying, she will be aware of it and be upset by it.'

I knew my words were hurting her as much as Martin's blows, but I had to try and get through to her.

'Hailey, there's research to show that babies can feel their mother's trauma in the womb and that it can affect their development when they're born.'

I could see that Hailey was shocked by this but I needed her to know the truth, no matter how painful.

'You've seen Jasmine since she's come to live with me,' I told her. 'She's moving around and making noise, she smiles and she cries. Can you see how different she looks? She's putting on weight and thriving. She wasn't doing any of that when she was living with you.'

It was all starting to make a lot of sense. Poor Jasmine was probably so frightened at home that she had stayed as still and as silent as possible.

'Look how different she was the other week in the contact sessions when you weren't there and Martin was. She cried all the time and she had to come back early because she was so distressed. She's just as frightened and anxious as you are, Hailey. Although he may never have hurt her, she can pick up on everything that's going on around her.'

As hard as this was, it needed to be said. Hailey had been desperately trying to convince herself that Jasmine was fine for so long, but that was far from the truth.

'Hailey, if you're scared to go home I can ring Claire now, explain what you've told me, and we can sort out a refuge for you to go to,' I told her. 'Just say the word and I'll pick up the phone. We will find you somewhere to go away from Martin where you'll be safe.'

'I can't,' she wept, clearly terrified. 'Wherever I go he'll find me. I know he will. He'll find me and he'll hurt me.'

I felt sick and utterly helpless. My heart went out to this poor, poor woman having to live in fear and despair 24/7.

'I have to go back,' she exclaimed, suddenly getting up. 'He'll want to know what happened today. He likes to know every single detail otherwise I'll get it in the neck just like I did last week.'

I hated the idea of letting her go back to this monster but in reality there was nothing I could do. It was her choice and I was powerless to stop her. Hailey was an adult and it was her daughter who was in the care system, not her.

I could see that after all her revelations, Hailey was exhausted and I didn't want to press her any more. I ordered her another taxi and gave her some money to pay for it.

'He'll want to know why I'm late back, Maggie,' she said, worry etched on her face. 'What am I going to tell him?'

'Just tell him the taxi didn't turn up and I had to order you another one and it was a bit of a wait,' I replied. 'Do you want me to help you take the bandage off your arm?'

I didn't want to do anything to inflame Martin and cause Hailey to be hurt further. She nodded meekly.

'Please look after yourself, Hailey,' I said, as I unwrapped the dressing, her burns angry and inflamed. 'See you next week.'

She nodded, bending to give Jasmine a goodbye kiss.

'Thank you, Maggie,' she said. 'For everything.'

I picked Jasmine up from the play mat and cuddled her as I stood by the front window, watching the taxi drive off down the road.

'You poor little thing,' I whispered, stroking the soft downy hairs in the nape of her neck. 'I can only imagine the things you must have seen.'

I couldn't stop thinking about all the fear she must have experienced in her short little life.

I was churned up with worry and anguish for Hailey. Everything made sense now but I was still angry at myself for not realising what had been going on. Was she going to get into trouble with Martin for being late? Had I caused her more problems? If I reported it to Claire would it put her in even more danger? It was horrendous to think that she had to go home and share a bed with that man. He wasn't a man, he was a monster. I'd never forgive myself if she got a beating because of the questions that I'd asked.

No matter what my concerns were, though, I knew that I had a responsibility to do the right thing. With a heavy heart, I picked up my mobile and rang Claire. It felt like a betrayal of Hailey's trust but I had no choice. I was responsible for Jasmine's welfare, and this information was crucial to that.

'I need to talk to you about something urgently,' I told Claire when she answered. 'Hailey came round for her session today and as she was washing up, I saw burns on her arm.

'She said she'd hurt herself on the oven but I've seen enough burns in my time to know they were done by a cigarette.

'There was a whole row of them right up her arm, Claire, and she also had bruising around her neck.'

'Oh gosh, the poor girl,' she sighed. 'Did you talk to her about how they'd happened?'

'I did,' I said. 'She broke down and eventually she admitted that it was Martin. She told me that he regularly hurts her.

'She insisted that he's never been violent to Jasmine, though. She was desperate for me not to tell you. Honestly, Claire, she was terrified.'

'That's horrific,' sighed Claire. 'I knew he was controlling but I never thought it was physical. No wonder Jasmine was so frozen and quiet when she first came to you. That also explains why she was getting so distressed in the contact sessions with Dad. We both know that babies are so sensitive to what's going on around them.'

'So what do we do now?' I asked. 'I honestly don't know where we go from here.

'Hailey was so frightened at the thought that Martin might find out she'd told me. She's terrified of him and what he might do to her. I did offer to call you and said we could sort out a place in a refuge as soon as possible but she refused.'

'Maggie, I honestly don't know,' Claire replied, sounding as grim as I felt. 'Let me talk this through with my manager. I'll get her advice and ring you straight back.'

I still felt guilty about betraying Hailey's trust but I knew I'd never forgive myself if something happened to her. My mind whirred as I paced up and down my living room waiting for Claire's call.

'It's a tough one,' she said, as I pounced on the phone. 'Because the baby's with you she's safe, so there isn't a child protection issue.

'But you and I both know we would never return a child to a household where there is violence.

'Now we know what's going on at home there's no point in us continuing with the parenting assessment, but we can't just cancel it as Martin will want to know why. That would put Hailey at risk and we have to protect her as much as possible.

'So what we need to do is make sure that you document everything that she's told you today and then I will have a chat to her myself.'

Claire wanted to get a full account of when and how Martin had hurt Hailey.

'Sadly I think it's been going on for years,' I sighed.

Together we came up with a plan.

'Let's keep the parenting assessment going as it is for now,' Claire told me. 'It's always supervised so Martin is never on his own with Jasmine.

'Next week I'll come along to Hailey's session at your house,' she went on. 'You and I need a good chunk of time with her on her own so we can all talk so I'll tell Jan she's not needed. Is there any way you can get somebody to have the baby that morning so there are no distractions?'

'Louisa will be at work but I can ask my friend Vicky,' I replied.

'Thanks,' she said. 'I think it's important you're there too. I think she's more likely to open up to you.'

'OK,' I said. 'I honestly don't know how she's going to react when she's confronted about it, but we can try.'

'Thank you for telling me, Maggie,' said Claire. 'You've done the right thing.'

I knew she was right, but it didn't stop me from feeling anxious. All week I worried that somehow Martin was going to find out what Hailey had told me and she was going to get the brunt of his anger. I was also anxious about how the contact sessions were going since all this had come out. Claire had briefed Jan, as she was leading the sessions and needed to be alert to anything worrying. Every time Jan dropped Jasmine back, I waited nervously to quiz her.

'Was everything OK today?' I asked. 'Was Mum there? How did she seem?'

'Hailey was there,' she replied. 'She was very quiet but that's no different from normal.'

'Did you notice any injuries on her?'

'Nothing that I could see,' she said. 'I didn't see any obvious bruises or marks, but she kept her scarf on and she was wearing a baggy jumper and jeans so it's impossible to know what's underneath.

'Don't worry, Maggie, I'm keeping an eye on it.'

Over the years I had dealt with a lot of domestic violence cases, as sadly it is a common reason why children are taken into care. However, I had never before been the person who had exposed the violence or the one the victim had opened up to. It made me feel responsible for her and her safety.

For confidentiality reasons I couldn't tell Vicky or Louisa about what was happening.

'There have been some new developments with Hailey,' I said to Vicky over a cuppa later that week. 'The social worker really needs to talk to her, but Hailey only talks openly if I'm there, so would you mind having Jasmine for a couple of hours next week?'

'Of course,' Vicky said. 'You know I'm happy to help. I hope everything's OK.'

'Me too,' I said sadly. And I meant that with all my heart.

I couldn't help but worry, though. All I could think about was Hailey's safety, and I wondered whether she was ever going to get Jasmine back.

TEN

Home Truths

On the day of Hailey's session at my house, I felt sick with nerves. How was she going to react when she realised Claire was here and that I'd obviously told her everything? What would happen if she clammed up and refused to talk?

When I heard the knock at the door, I took a deep breath.

'It's going to be OK, Maggie,' Claire told me reassuringly.

When I opened it and Hailey saw Claire stood behind me, her face dropped. She took three steps backwards back onto the front path.

'What have you said?' she screamed. 'What did you tell her?'

'Hailey, I explained to you last week that I had to tell Claire what you told me. For Jasmine's sake I couldn't keep it a secret.'

'I begged you,' she said, her eyes filling with tears. 'He's going to know I said something now and he's going to kill me. And that will be your fault. That will be on your conscience.'

She burst into tears.

'Hailey, come on in and we'll all sit down and talk about this,' Claire urged her.

'I've not come to talk to you,' she snapped. 'I've come to see my baby.'

She pushed past us and stormed into the living room. Then she dashed into the kitchen. She stood there, staring at the empty high chair.

'Where is she?' she shrieked. 'Where's Jasmine?'

'Jasmine is absolutely fine,' I told her. 'Another foster carer is looking after her while we talk.'

'Are you stopping me from seeing her?' she asked, looking terrified.

'Nobody's stopping you from seeing your baby, Hailey. We just felt it was important that we had some time with you without any distractions,' said Claire.

'Does Martin know?' she stammered. 'Does he know what I told Maggie?'

Claire shook her head, trying to reassure her. 'For now, this is a confidential discussion between the three of us. Maggie and I just want to try and understand what's been going on at home.'

Claire had told me that she wanted to speak to Hailey alone first, so I made myself scarce while they talked in the living room. Although I knew I had been obliged to share what Hailey had confided in me, I still felt so guilty about it. I just hoped that Claire had managed to calm Hailey down. Ten minutes later, Claire came into the kitchen to find me.

'How's it going?' I asked.

'I'm not getting anywhere, Maggie. She's upset and she's not saying anything. She won't open up to me at all. It's hopeless.'

'Do you want me to try and talk to her?' I asked, and she nodded.

Hailey was curled up in a ball on the sofa, silently sobbing. She literally looked like she had withdrawn into herself. I went and sat down next to her.

'Hailey, I know you must be really scared and I can't imagine how hard this is for you, but for Jasmine's sake you need to tell Claire what has been going on,' I urged her, as gently as I could.

'Remember when I saw the bruises on your neck and the burns on your arm last week?'

Hailey nodded.

'Tell me again how you got those.'

'You know how I got them,' she mumbled, her face still shielded by her hands.

'I do,' I said. 'But Claire needs to hear it too. Who hurt you, Hailey?'

'Martin did,' she whimpered. 'Martin did it because he was angry with me. That's why I couldn't come to contact.'

'Has he hurt you before?' I asked.

She nodded her head and I could see her bottom lip quivering.

'All the time,' she said. 'He gets cross if I do something I shouldn't.'

'What things do you do that you shouldn't?' I asked her gently.

She couldn't stop the tears from flowing now. I edged closer to her and held her hand.

'I know this is so hard for you, Hailey, but you need to tell us what's really been happening at home.'

Then suddenly it was as if the floodgates had opened. Finally, at long last, Hailey began to talk.

★

With every word that she spoke, the truth came tumbling out for the very first time. All I could do was listen and hold her hand as she told us what Martin had subjected her to.

'It's not him hurting me that's the worst,' she said, in between gulping sobs. 'I can handle the pain, I'm used to it. It's all the other stuff.

'He won't let me pick Jasmine up even when she cries,' she told us. 'I'm only allowed to when I have his permission.

'He watches me all the time and he won't let me talk to her or play with her or even cuddle her. He doesn't believe babies should have toys or new clothes.'

She described how Jasmine was only allowed to wear second-hand clothes that he had found at charity shops.

'Even when she's crying for a bottle he won't let me feed her until he says it's time. And when I did give her a bottle he timed me, and if she hadn't drunk it all in a few minutes then he'd throw it away and not let her have any more.

'He said I was overfeeding her and he didn't want her to get fat.'

Claire and I gave each other a knowing look. That explained why Jasmine had been dangerously underweight when she was taken into care.

'I wasn't even allowed to go to her in the night when she was crying,' she continued. 'It was torture lying there, hearing her sobbing and getting more and more worked up.

'Then after a while she stopped and that was almost worse. She stopped crying because she realised it was pointless, that no one would come and comfort her. So she did this quiet sort of wailing noise instead but I could still hear it. It broke my heart.'

She started to cry again.

'You're doing so well, Hailey,' I told her. 'Just take your time.'

She gulped down her tears and caught her breath.

'I thought it would be OK because Jasmine and I would have the daytimes to be together. But since he lost his job he's there every minute, breathing down my neck, watching me. There's no escape.

'One night he didn't wake up when she cried so I got up and went to her. It was so lovely being able to cuddle her and talk to her. But then he woke up.

'I learnt my lesson that day. He kicked and punched me and rubbed a dirty nappy in my face.'

I was horrified. I couldn't help but be shocked by the horrendous things Hailey was telling us. My heart went out to poor little Jasmine, too, born into this environment of fear and violence.

While Hailey was talking, Claire was quietly taking notes and documenting it all.

'Tell me how he hurts you,' I asked her gently.

'Kicks, punches, slaps; he pulls my hair, burns me with cigarettes, puts his hands around my neck and strangles me.

'He's thrown me against a wall a couple of times and threatened me with a knife.'

She said it so matter-of-factly, as though she was reading out a shopping list.

'But I swear to you that he's never ever done it when I've been holding Jasmine, and he's never done anything to her,' she said firmly. 'I told him if he hurt her then I would kill him and I would. I really would.'

I didn't doubt it.

'How long has this been going on for, Hailey?' I asked her. She shrugged.

'Since just after we got together,' she replied. 'I met him when I was fifteen, and I'm 23 now.

'He said he'd look after me and that I didn't need to work, so I gave up my plans to go to college.

'He didn't want me working in an office where there were other men around, because he said he couldn't trust me. I was dependent on him for money and somewhere to live.

'Martin told me I didn't deserve new clothes so he chooses them from charity shops. Mostly he gets me men's stuff. Even my shoes are men's.'

I could see the shame in her face as she told us all this.

'It never used to be this bad,' she continued. 'Just the odd punch or slap now and again if I did something wrong.

'Sometimes he'd be nice to me but since Jasmine was born it's got a lot worse. He tells me that I'm a terrible mum, that I can't look after Jasmine properly and that she hates me.

'Anyway, why wouldn't she hate me?' she sobbed. 'I've let her down. I've left her to lie in her cot all day and ignored her when she cried.'

I could see by her face that she really believed him. I felt so awful for this poor girl to have had to live through eight long years of hell.

'What happened the other week when you missed your assessment sessions?' I asked gently. 'Were you really ill?'

Hailey shook her head.

'He laid into me because he said I wasn't telling him the truth about what had happened at the session I had here at your house.

'He was so angry with me. He said he bet I'd been talking too much and picking Jasmine up and spoiling her and he hadn't given me permission.

'He held down my arm and burnt me with his cigarette and tried to strangle me. Then he kicked me so hard I was doubled up in agony. I couldn't get out of bed for days.'

'I'm so, so sorry, Hailey,' I said. And I meant every word.

I was utterly appalled at what Martin had put her through. The only positive was that at least we now knew the truth and it answered many of our questions about Jasmine's behaviour.

'Hailey, you don't have to put up with this,' I told her. 'You're worth far more than this. Your baby is worth far more.

'You have to think seriously about leaving him.'

But I knew it was easy for me to say. Martin had been in Hailey's life since she was a teenager. The violence and the fear were ingrained in her; they had become part of normal life.

'We're asking you to tell us all this because we want to protect you,' I carried on. 'I know you desperately want to get Jasmine back but that's not going to happen while you're living with someone that hurts you.'

'Oh no, it's fine,' said Hailey. 'Jasmine can come back home. I told you, he doesn't touch her, I won't let him.'

I couldn't believe what I was hearing, and I was struck by how naive she was being.

'But what happens if one day he does?' asked Claire. 'What happens if you're holding the baby when Martin attacks you, and he misses his target and hurts her instead?

'What if he beats you so badly that you're unconscious. How could you ensure Jasmine is safe then?'

'Hailey, it's not just about Martin hurting Jasmine. It's about the effect that living in an environment of fear has on her, and how damaging that is for her development.'

Hailey dissolved into tears again. She sat there sobbing while Claire and I exchanged grim looks. I felt terrible for Hailey but she needed to know the truth.

'What happens now?' she asked, drying her eyes with the tatty sleeve of her jumper. 'What are you going to do?'

'Well, we know Jasmine's safe here with Maggie, and Martin is never on his own with her,' said Claire. 'So at this point in time I'm more concerned about you and your safety.'

'You're not going to tell him, though, are you?' asked Hailey, the panic rising in her voice. 'You can't tell him that you know what he does to me.'

'I honestly don't know what we're going to do, but nothing's going to happen straight away,' Claire replied. 'I appreciate you being so honest with us, and now I need to go away and have a meeting with my managers and try and decide the best way forward.

'What I would say, Hailey, is while we're doing that you need to have a long hard think about what you want your life to be like. Do you want to stay with your husband, or do you want to have a chance at getting your daughter back?

'Because the harsh reality is, you need to choose. It's got to be one or the other.'

Hailey started to cry again and I could see she was shell-shocked. I left her curled up on the sofa as I walked out into the hallway with Claire.

'I'll be in touch and let you know how we're going to proceed,' Claire said. 'Until then, as we discussed, everything will continue as normal.'

'OK,' I replied, 'I'll keep an eye on her.'

I returned to the living room. Hailey hadn't moved from the sofa and remained curled up in a foetal position.

'You were very brave to tell us all that,' I said, taking her hand in mine. 'I'm going to go and make us a cup of tea and then I'm going to phone Vicky to see if she can drop Jasmine back here. I think you could do with a cuddle from your baby.'

Hailey nodded, her eyes red raw from tears.

'I'd like that,' she smiled, meekly.

I arranged for Vicky to drop Jasmine around as soon as she could.

Carrying two cuppas back into the lounge, I could see Hailey was still very teary and frightened.

'I should never have said anything,' she wept. 'I'm so scared about what's going to happen, Maggie.'

'Hailey, you did the right thing,' I told her. 'At least this way we can try and help you and Jasmine.'

But she didn't look convinced. When Vicky turned up, Jasmine was fast asleep in her car seat.

'Is everything OK?' Vicky asked when she saw Hailey's face puffy and swollen with tears.

'It will be,' I smiled.

Hailey rushed over to her daughter and stroked her cheek.

'I'm so sorry, Jasmine,' she told her, scooping her up into her arms. 'I don't want to lose you.'

It was almost too painful to watch. I let her have some quiet time on her own with the baby. Thankfully after an hour with

Jasmine, Hailey had calmed down. However, I could see she was exhausted and still in shock about what had happened. When the time the taxi came to take her home, I gave her a hug.

'Please look after yourself,' I told her. But I knew that with a brute like Martin, that was easier said than done.

Over the next few days Hailey was constantly on my mind. I felt so responsible for her. I'd forced her into telling us what Martin did to her and I knew I'd never forgive myself if something happened to her. As I was washing up one night, I couldn't stop going over the horrific details of what Martin had done to her. I couldn't imagine living with that fear and violence day in, day out. How on earth had the poor woman coped?

Louisa must have noticed my worried look.

'Is everything all right, Maggie?' she asked. 'You seem a bit down, like you've got something on your mind.'

'There is something, lovey,' I said. 'There's a lot happening with Jasmine's mum and dad that unfortunately I can't discuss with you. But we'll work it out. It's just a bit of a worrying time.'

She'd been with me long enough to know that because of confidentiality reasons I couldn't discuss the intricacies of cases with her.

'I'll babysit if you want to have a night out with Graham,' she said. 'Maybe that would help.'

Graham. I felt a stab of guilt that with the events of the past few weeks, I'd neglected him.

'It's OK,' I sighed. 'I don't really feel like going out at the minute. Graham's probably fed up of me but hopefully he understands.'

With all this going on at home, I just didn't feel very sociable.

There was also the twins' adoption to start thinking about. A few days later, Helen, their adoption worker, rang to update me. She sounded very chirpy.

'I've got some good news for you, Maggie,' she said.

'Oh, that makes a nice change,' I laughed.

'I went round to see Lizzie and Joe, the couple who were potentially interested in adopting Polly and Daisy,' she told me. 'They were absolutely lovely. I gave them a bit of a potted history about the girls and their background, and they seem really keen.'

'That's great,' I replied. 'So what happens next?'

'I'd like to come round and meet the twins myself and perhaps take some photos and a little film of them on my phone so I can show Lizzie and Joe. Would that be OK?'

'Of course,' I said. 'Come round any day after school.'

I was pleased that this couple were keen to adopt Polly and Daisy, but I also hoped that they were truly aware of the realities of adopting two children who had been badly neglected. There was no doubt the girls had come on in leaps and bounds, and were unrecognisable from the two little terrified mites who had come to live with me. But when children suffer such cruel neglect for the first few years, there can be ramifications for the rest of their lives. None of us could predict how it would affect them in the future and it could cause all sorts of issues with their attachment, schooling, relationships and behaviour.

When Helen came round the following afternoon to meet the girls, we had a chat in the kitchen first.

'What a lovely baby,' she said, as I sat with Jasmine on my knee. 'And so smiley.'

'Yes, she's just started doing that,' I laughed. She was now such a stark contrast to the baby that had come to live with me three months ago.

Jasmine had just mastered sitting up, so I put her on some foam tiles on the kitchen floor, surrounded by cushions in case she wobbled and fell back.

'How are the twins getting on?' Helen asked.

'They're fine,' I said. 'We've been talking lots more about forever families and we've been reading books about new mummies and daddies. They seem happy with it all but I'm being very cautious and keeping a close eye on them.'

'Do you think they're ready, or do we need to put things on hold for now?' she asked.

'I think they're ready as they'll ever be,' I replied. 'I'm just mindful of everything they've been through in the past, and it isn't going to be a quick fix. It's going to take them years to work through the anger and the pain of what happened to them.

'I'm anxious that any prospective parents are aware of that, too, and are not just swept away with the idea of two beautiful little twins. I want them to be going into this adoption with their eyes open.'

'I understand what you're saying,' Helen reassured me. 'And I share your concerns. I will be talking a lot to Lizzie and Joe and we'll be doing lots of work with them about how trauma can manifest itself in children and how to deal with it.'

After she'd had a cup of tea I took her into the living room to meet the twins.

'Girls, there's someone here to meet you,' I told them. 'This is Helen.'

'Are you our new mummy?' Polly asked her hopefully.

Bless her, I thought to myself. She really had taken all this talk of new mummies and daddies to heart.

'No, darling, sadly I'm not,' she said. 'But it's my job to talk to all the mummies and daddies who want you to come and live with them and I'm going to pick the best ones for you.

'Then I'm going to tell them all about you both and how brilliant you are.'

Helen spent the next half an hour chatting to the girls about what they liked to eat, their favourite toys and what they liked to do.

'I like building towers with Duplo,' said Polly. 'And Daisy likes drawing.'

'Yeah, and I'm really good at writing my name,' added Daisy.

'I want to ride a bike and have a green helmet,' continued Polly. 'And I love fish and chips.'

'Well, I shall make sure that I pass all that on to your new mummy and daddy,' smiled Helen.

At five the twins were old enough to retain clear memories of their birth parents and they would regularly remember things and ask questions. All this talk of new mummies and daddies was stirring up old memories for them.

That night over dinner Daisy suddenly announced: 'Mummy didn't give us any food yesterday so me and Polly had to eat the cat's food.'

'Yeah, it was stinky and yucky,' grimaced Polly.

'Sweetie, that didn't happen yesterday,' I told her. 'That was a long time ago when you lived at your tummy mummy's house, wasn't it?'

'Well, I like your dinners, Maggie,' said Daisy. 'Our old mummy didn't cook dinners. Will our new mummy cook dinners or will we have to have the cat's yucky food again?'

'I think your new mummy and daddy will cook lovely dinners,' I smiled. 'And I'll make sure that we tell them all your favourites.'

I knew any change was going to be unsettling for the girls. They'd already been through so much in their short lives and I was going to spend the next few weeks reassuring them as much as I could.

That night when all three children were in bed, I slumped onto the sofa. I felt exhausted and my head was spinning.

Fostering was a constant juggling act and I was dealing with so many conflicting emotions.

On the one hand, I had the twins who were hopefully about to start one of the happiest, most exciting journeys of getting a new mummy and daddy, yet at the same time it was also very emotional for them and a time of huge upheaval. Then on the other I had Jasmine, who was potentially facing one of the saddest times and having to say goodbye to her birth mummy.

I had become adept in the art of plate spinning and balancing different children's needs at the same time. But sometimes, like all parents, I was consumed by worries. As foster carers, we are taught to be unemotional and detached, but the reality of being a foster carer is completely different. It was impossible for me not to get attached to the children in my care. I invested in every child who came through my front door, and I wanted the best for all of them. I just hoped I was doing right by Jasmine.

★

Five days after Hailey had revealed the truth to us, Claire rang.

'I had a meeting with my managers and we discussed all the issues that have come to light,' she said. 'I'm going to come round when Hailey has her next session at your house and talk to you both about it then. Is that OK?'

'That's absolutely fine,' I said.

Because we couldn't alert Martin to what was happening, Claire couldn't ring Hailey and let her know what was going on. I doubted that she even had a phone as none of us had a mobile number for her and Social Services only had Martin's. There was no choice but to wait until the weekly session she had at my house. I couldn't stop myself from worrying about her and wondering what was going on at home. I just prayed that Hailey was OK.

When she turned up, I found myself anxiously looking her up and down, trying to spot any new bruises or injuries.

'How are your burns?' I asked her. 'Have you been keeping them clean?'

'They're fine,' she said, not looking at me.

I could see she felt ashamed that we now knew what Martin did to her.

'How are things at home?' asked Claire.

Hailey shrugged.

'I've been worried sick that you're going to say something to him,' she said.

'We promised we wouldn't, Hailey,' Claire told her. 'We've decided to keep the assessment going for another four weeks. Until then we will keep what you've told us confidential and we won't say anything to Martin.'

'Thank God,' sighed Hailey, relief washing over her.

'That gives you a month to make a decision about what you want to do before we cancel the assessment,' added Claire.

'Social Services has to be transparent with parents, so when we cancel it we will have to give your husband a valid reason why. We will have to make him aware that we know about the domestic violence and I will have to make a recommendation that Jasmine can't be returned home because of this.'

I knew this was going to break Hailey, but it was the only way forward.

'You've got four weeks to spend time with Jasmine, talk to Maggie if you want and decide what you want to do,' Claire continued.

'Above all, you need be aware that if you do decide to stay with Martin then your baby won't be coming back to live with you, and in all likelihood we'll start the adoption process.'

Hailey needed to know the harsh reality of what would happen if she stayed in this relationship.

Hailey's face crumpled and she started to cry. I moved closer to her on the sofa, and took her hand in mine.

'The alternative is that we can help you if you want us to. We can find you a safe place to go and we can sort out accommodation for you away from Martin.'

'Then can I get my baby back?' Hailey asked, hopefully.

'Unfortunately it's not as simple as that,' Claire replied. 'If you want us to, we can start a parenting assessment with you on your own. And if that goes well, and you can convince us that you are permanently living apart from Martin, then we can look at returning Jasmine to your care.

'The offer of help is there, but you have to be the one to make the move, Hailey. Maggie and I can't make that decision for you.'

Both of us knew we couldn't force her to leave Martin, but at least this plan gave her a bit of breathing space and time to make a decision.

Hailey looked terrified. After so many years of abuse, she was his prisoner – mentally and physically.

'When you cancel the assessment and he finds out why, he's going to kill me,' she said. 'He's always said the only way I'll leave him is in a coffin. What if he's right?'

Her words sent a shiver down my spine.

'Hailey, if you decide to leave Martin we'll do everything we can to protect you and Jasmine,' Claire said. 'There are places you can go that are secure where he can't find you.'

'But what if he does?' she pleaded, her blue eyes wide with fear.

'He won't, Hailey,' I cut in. 'You have to trust us.'

I just hoped she would. Up until this point, Martin was the only one she could depend on, and she was completely under his control. She was terrified to be with him and terrified to be without him.

But we had to show her she could depend on us. We had to get her to see that this was ultimately a simple choice: Martin or her baby. But what we didn't know was whether this decision would be ruled by fear or by love.

ELEVEN

Decision Time

As much as I would have liked to, the reality was that I couldn't make the decision for Hailey. She had to do it for herself. Over the next few weeks, all I could do was to try and make her realise what she would be missing out on if she decided to stay with Martin.

I also wanted to try and boost her self-confidence as much as I could. I could tell that any self-esteem she'd ever had had been beaten out of her over the years, as it is for many women who suffer domestic violence. She was terrified to be with Martin but at the same time she was also terrified of being without him.

It was obvious that the mental anguish was taking its toll on Hailey. When she arrived at my house the following week after our conversation with Claire, she looked like she'd hardly slept. She seemed utterly exhausted.

'Is Jan coming later?' she asked.

'Claire's agreed that there's no point in her coming to these sessions any more as we know the assessment's going to be cancelled anyway,' I told her. 'So the next few weeks will give you a bit of breathing space. It's a chance for you to spend time with Jasmine and to talk things through with me.

'That's only if you want to, of course.'

'I'm so sorry for causing problems, Maggie,' she said sadly. 'I never meant for any of this to happen.'

'There's absolutely no need for you to apologise,' I replied. 'You're not the problem here. The problem is that you're being hurt and we want to try and help you find a way out of it. You are a victim – you need to understand that.'

I could see how scared Hailey was and how daunting the idea of leaving Martin seemed to her. It could be hard to understand a toxic relationship like Hailey's and Martin's if you'd never experienced it. Someone was offering Hailey a way out, and it was easy to feel frustrated and wonder why she didn't just take the chance to leave him.

But I knew from dealing with other women who had experienced domestic abuse that unfortunately it wasn't as simple as that. Hailey had met Martin when she was practically a child herself, and over time he'd isolated her from her friends and family and cut her off from society so she was totally and utterly dependent on him. She spent every waking hour with him.

It was what psychologists refer to as Stockholm Syndrome – where people develop a dependence on their captors, even though they're treated appallingly.

'Do you enjoy having time with Jasmine here without him?' I asked Hailey.

She nodded meekly.

'I spend all week looking forward to these few hours,' she smiled. 'It's what keeps me going. I feel so free not having him breathing down my neck and I don't have to ask permission to touch my own daughter. I love being able to play with her and talk to her and just cuddle her whenever I want.'

She tickled Jasmine under her chin, and as if on cue Jasmine gave her a big gummy grin.

'And look how much she enjoys spending time with her mummy too,' I smiled. 'Just imagine, Hailey, you could feel like that all the time.'

But I'm not sure she truly believed she could do it. I desperately wanted to make her see how much she had to lose if she stayed with Martin, even if that meant having to be cruel to be kind.

While Hailey fed Jasmine her lunch, I ironed the twins' school uniform. Jasmine was slowly starting to try a little bit of pureed food now.

'Oh, look at their little pinafores,' sighed Hailey. 'They're really cute.'

'They are,' I said, showing her their little white blouses with the scalloped collars and the buttons shaped like flowers.

'Imagine when it's Jasmine's first day at school,' I said. 'Would you like to be there for that?'

Hailey looked shocked and then her face crumpled.

I knew it was tough for her to hear but it was also the truth, and Hailey needed to think through the implications of her decision. If she stayed with Martin, there were so many things she'd miss out on. She wouldn't be there to see her daughter's first steps, or hold her hand on her first day at school, or be a proud mum on her wedding day.

Hailey started to cry.

'I do want to be there, Maggie,' she sobbed. 'I can't bear to think of not being there. But it's not as simple as that.'

I put the iron down and went and sat with her.

'I don't want to upset you, Hailey,' I said. 'I know you think I'm being horrible saying all this, but it's important for you to realise what you're potentially giving up.

'The choice has got to be yours,' I told her, looking straight into her eyes. 'None of us can make it for you.'

'I know, Maggie,' she wept. 'I want to leave him but I'm just not sure I'm strong enough.'

'If you do decide to stay with him, at the end of this four weeks, one way or another, Martin's going to find out why we're cancelling this assessment.

'Imagine you both going to the meeting when Claire raises these issues. At the end of it you will have to leave and go home with him. What will happen then?'

'He'll kill me,' she said matter of factly.

'Well, then, do you want to leave Jasmine without a mother?'

It sounded like a cruel thing for me to say but it was the reality she was facing. Social Services had offered Hailey a way out, but if she didn't take it they were unlikely to be able to offer her any more protection. They might decide to pass their concerns on to the police but they weren't under any obligation. She was a grown adult and was capable of making her own decisions and they couldn't interfere with that.

'I know the idea of leaving him must feel terrifying but perhaps in reality it would be more terrifying for you to stay.' I told her gently.

'My head's spinning,' she sobbed. 'I keep going over and over it in my mind and I just don't know what to do.'

I could see she was stressed and I decided not to talk about it any more this session. Just before she left Hailey asked if she could feed Jasmine her bottle.

'Of course you can. Because she's eating a bit more food now I've reduced her bottles from six ounces to three,' I told her.

Hailey got on with giving Jasmine her milk while I carried on with the ironing.

'Gosh, she's taking her time over that,' I said as she fed her. 'She normally gulps down three ounces in a few minutes.'

Hailey's face fell.

'Oh no,' she said. 'I got it wrong. I gave her six ounces like before, and not three like you said. I didn't listen. Martin's always telling me I don't listen. I'm so sorry, Maggie.'

She looked utterly dejected.

'Hailey, it doesn't matter,' I said. 'She loves her milk and three extra ounces are not going to do her any harm.'

She broke down and started sobbing.

'I can't do this, Maggie,' she cried. 'He's right. I *am* useless. Jasmine's better off without me.'

'That's complete and utter nonsense,' I said firmly. 'You're a good mum and you know exactly what your daughter needs.'

I felt so angry with Martin that he had manipulated her into believing his lies.

'I don't think I can do it on my own,' she sighed. 'I'm not strong enough. What if she cries all the time when she's with me? I don't have any friends, my family don't live nearby. I've got no one.'

'You wouldn't be on your own,' I replied. 'If you went to a refuge there are people there whose job it is to support you.

There are all sorts of things in these places, like mother-and-baby groups, and you'd be offered counselling.

'I'm still going to be here. You can still visit Jasmine, and Claire and I will support you.'

All her worries and fears came tumbling out.

'But what if I leave him and then I don't pass the assessment?'

'I'm not going to lie to you, Hailey, there are no guarantees,' I told her. 'You would have to convince Social Services that Martin was completely out of your life for good.

'But from what I've seen of your parenting, my feeling is that you would sail through any assessment.'

'But what if I mess up like I did with the milk?'

'Nobody's perfect,' I said. 'We all make mistakes from time to time. Anyone would if their parenting was being put under a microscope, but there's nothing you have done here with the baby that has worried me. Feeding her an extra three ounces of milk hasn't done her any harm.

'You're totally and completely natural with her and you know how to look after her. Above all of that, I can see how much you love her.'

But was love going to be enough?

As Hailey got ready to leave, I carried Jasmine to the door while she put her shoes on. Jasmine started to cry and she reached over and held her arms out to Hailey.

'I think she wants her mummy,' I said.

'She wants me?' gasped Hailey, looking surprised. 'But she lives with you. You look after her, you're with her all the time. Why does she want me?'

'Because you're her mum,' I said.

'She doesn't remember me,' Hailey replied. My heart went out to her.

'Of course she does,' I said. 'Babies know their mums. They recognise their smell and their voice and the way it feels when you hold them in your arms.'

In fostering we use the term 'the invisible umbilical cord' to describe that unbreakable bond between a mother and her baby. Even though I was Jasmine's main care giver, there was a familiarity about Hailey even after a few months of living apart. Jasmine instinctively knew how her mum held her, and she'd heard her voice from when she was in the womb. I just hoped this bond was strong enough to overcome the power Martin held over Hailey.

The sessions at the family centre were still continuing and on three mornings a week Jan came to pick up Jasmine. On the day of one of Martin's individual sessions, I was surprised when the doorbell rang and I opened the door to find Jan standing there with Jasmine. She'd only been gone twenty minutes.

'What happened?' I asked.

'Dad didn't turn up,' she replied. 'No phone call. No nothing. He just didn't show.'

'Why would he do that?' I asked.

I couldn't believe Martin would do anything to jeopardise the assessment.

'I think as time goes on he's embarrassed that Jasmine still cries throughout the whole session and she won't go to him,' she said. 'If he picks her up then she leans over and reaches out to me even though I'm practically a stranger.

'Claire has said if he's a no-show again then his individual session will be cancelled.'

I asked how the joint sessions were going.

'Jasmine is fine as long as Mum's there. Both she and Hailey are so much quieter than they are here. The atmosphere is always very stilted and tense but I can see Jasmine gets comfort from her mum.

'When Dad's around it's like Mum's walking on eggshells, and obviously now we all know why.'

The following week Hailey turned up for her session at my house wearing a pair of sunglasses. It was a cloudy November day and my heart sank when I saw her.

'Oh, Hailey,' I sighed. 'What's he done to you?'

She took off her glasses to reveal a black eye. She was so ashamed, she wouldn't look at me.

'What happened?' I asked.

'I turned the heating on when he went out to the shop without asking his permission,' she said.

I made her a cup of tea and didn't mention it again.

'Why aren't you saying anything about it to me, Maggie?' she asked. 'Are you cross with me?'

'There's nothing I *can* say,' I sighed. 'I'm not cross; I'm upset that he's hurt you again. It's awful, and you shouldn't be in this situation, but I'm powerless to make you do anything to change it.

'It's going to keep on happening, Hailey, and I suppose I'm curious as to why on earth you would choose to stay with a man who does this to you, rather than keep your daughter?'

'Because I'm scared,' she wept. 'If I leave him I'm terrified that he will find me and kill me. And he might hurt Jasmine too just to get back at me.'

All I could do was talk her through each of her fears and reassure her.

'Refuges are designed to protect vulnerable women like you,' I told her. 'They're very secure. Martin wouldn't know where you were, he wouldn't be able to track you down and you wouldn't have to see him.'

'But I don't think I could cope on my own,' she said. 'Being with him is all I've ever known.'

'You wouldn't be on your own, I promise you. You'd have lots of support around you.'

That morning's post arrived with an envelope of photos that I'd ordered.

'Come and have a look at these,' I said, spreading them out on the kitchen table so she could have a look.

'I got them done for Jasmine's memory book,' I said. 'I make one for every child I foster.'

They'd been taken over the past two and half months that Jasmine had been with me.

'Gosh, look how much she's grown,' I said.

'She was so tiny and pale,' sighed Hailey.

Most of the pictures were of Jasmine on her own and then a couple with the twins and Louisa. The child in the photos was almost unrecognisable from the happy, healthy baby she was now.

'We must get some photos of you with Jasmine,' I told her.

'Why?' asked Hailey, surprised.

'If she does go for adoption it's important that her book contains photos of her and her birth mummy. That will be important for her growing up.'

Hailey broke down again.

'I can't bear the thought of someone else loving her. Of her having a different mummy and growing up without me.'

'That doesn't have to happen,' I reminded her.

'Would she really be adopted, Maggie?' she asked suddenly. 'Is that really what would happen, or are you and Claire just saying that to frighten me?

'What if I can't leave him now but I decide to in a few months? Couldn't Jasmine just stay with you for a bit longer in case I change my mind?'

I couldn't believe she still hadn't grasped the seriousness of the situation. 'I'm afraid it doesn't work like that,' I said. 'Because of Jasmine's age it's important to try and settle her with a new family as soon as possible.

'When the assessment is cancelled Claire will start liaising with the adoption team to start off the process.

'It's not fair to keep a baby in foster care in the hope that its birth parents change their mind. And babies are normally very easy to place.'

'Could I still see her even if she'd been adopted?' asked Hailey.

I shook my head sadly.

'The most you could possibly hope for is a letter once a year,' I replied.

It was the bitter truth. Even if it was hard for her to hear it, Hailey had to know exactly what she was giving up.

One morning, Jan was off sick and couldn't collect Jasmine for the family session so I offered to take her instead. As I walked up to reception, my heart sank as I saw Hailey and Martin were already there.

I hadn't seen Martin for weeks since the review, and it was hard to be civil to someone you knew had caused someone so much hurt and pain. I found him utterly repellent but I knew I had to be polite in order to keep up appearances. Often, in cases like this, I found that I over-compensated – if anything I was too nice and cheerful.

Hailey, true to form in Martin's presence, had her head down, not speaking, too frightened to make eye contact with anyone. She looked up when I walked in and gave me a weak smile and I could see she'd tried to disguise her black eye with make-up.

'Oh, hello, Maggie,' smiled Martin. 'I haven't seen you for a while.'

'Hi,' I said breezily, flashing him a fake smile. 'How are you doing?'

'Great, everything's going really well isn't it?' he said, grabbing Hailey's hand. 'We'll soon have our baby home.'

It was incredibly tempting to catch Hailey's eye, but I didn't want to put her in a dangerous position so I was careful not to look at her. She had become an expert at keeping up a pretence.

I couldn't even stand being in the same room as Martin and I got out of there as quickly as I could. It was only when I got in the car and put my hands on the steering wheel that I realised they were shaking. I was shaking not with fear, but with utter rage and anger. Here was a man who believed that after the way he had hurt his partner his daughter was still going to come home. What did he think gave him the right to treat another human being like that?

I felt so overwhelmed with anger that I gave my link worker Becky a ring.

'Becky, have you got time to listen to me offload and have a moan?' I asked.

I told her what had happened and how repulsed and angry Martin made me feel.

'How can Hailey live with a man who does that to her?' I raged. 'To be honest, I just want to kill him. I feel so powerless, Becky.'

'We know what the right decision is but Hailey has to make it herself,' Becky's calming voice came down the line. 'But I can see how frustrating this must be for you, Maggie.'

I wanted to shake Hailey and ask her what on earth was she thinking, but deep down I knew I just had to let it happen and not interfere too much. As a foster carer, I have a natural urge to rescue people. Here was somebody who was in pain and had so much to lose. I found it dreadfully hard to sit back and just watch it happen.

It was now three weeks since Hailey had confessed to us the ugly truth of what had been going on at home. We were fast approaching her fourth and final sessions at my house. After that, she would have to make her decision. And at this point in time, I didn't honestly know which way it was going to go.

TWELVE

Battered and Broken

Tap, tap, tap.

I thought the noise was part of my dream. Then I realised it was actually happening in real life. I sat bolt upright in bed, heart pounding. All was quiet. Then I heard it again.

Tap, tap, tap.

It was quiet at first but then it got louder and more persistent. There was knocking on my front door.

I looked at the clock. It was 1 a.m.

Who on earth was knocking on my door at this time of the morning? Being a woman on my own, I felt uneasy about opening the door to anyone at this time of night. But I also didn't want them to carry on and wake up Louisa, Jasmine and the twins.

My heart was going ten to the dozen as I grabbed my dressing gown and padded downstairs.

'Who is it?' I asked softly through the glass.

No answer.

Maybe it was some teenagers playing a prank on their way home from a night out. Something told me I had to check, though.

Keeping the chain on, I nervously opened the door.

'Who is it?' I called, struggling to keep the fear out of my voice. 'Who's there?'

As I looked out into the pitch black, frosty night I couldn't see anyone at first. But as my eyes adjusted to the darkness, I looked down and realised that there was a figure curled up on the doorstep in the foetal position.

'Help me,' a voice moaned. 'Please help me, Maggie.'

It was then that I realised with complete and utter horror who it was.

'Oh my God, Hailey,' I gasped. 'What's happened to you?'

I knew I had to get her inside. She was so frail and slight I managed to sit her up and somehow drag her into the hallway, where she collapsed onto the floor.

Seeing her in the light, my heart sank. She had been so badly beaten she was practically unrecognisable. Her nose was bloody, bruised and swollen and she had two black eyes. She was wearing what looked like baggy men's pyjamas and the top was soaked in blood. She was shivering and shaking and breathing very heavily. It was a cold night and God knows how long she had been lying there on the doorstep. In her state, it was a miracle that she had even managed to summon up the energy to knock.

Martin. Every curse word under the sun went through my head in that moment.

'What has he done to you?' I raged.

'I'm sorry, Maggie, I didn't know where else to go,' she croaked, and as she spoke, blood bubbled from the corner of her mouth. 'I thought he was going to kill me.'

'Don't try and talk,' I urged her. 'Take deep breaths.

'It's going to be OK. I'm going to call an ambulance and we're going to get you to hospital.'

I crouched down next to her on the floor. My hands were shaking as I dialled 999 on my mobile.

'I need an ambulance please,' I gabbled, giving the operator my address. 'Please come quickly.'

I was trying to stay calm for Hailey's sake but inside I was panicking. It was hard not to. She looked in such a bad way. There was blood everywhere and her breathing was really laboured.

Please hurry up, I repeated in my head, willing the ambulance to arrive.

She was still freezing so I ran and got her a blanket from the sofa in the living room and covered her with it.

'Hailey, I've got to leave you for two minutes while I go and speak to Louisa,' I said. 'But I'm coming back, OK?'

She nodded before her head slumped forward again.

I dashed upstairs and stuck my head around Jasmine's door. Mercifully she was curled up in her cot fast asleep. When I checked on the twins they were asleep too and I was grateful none of them had woken up in the commotion. Then I crept into Louisa's room and gently shook her awake.

'I'm sorry to disturb you, love,' I whispered. 'Jasmine's mum is downstairs. She's been badly hurt and I need to take her to hospital.'

'What?' she asked groggily, sitting up in bed. 'What's happened?'

'I've got to take Jasmine's mum to hospital,' I repeated. 'Jasmine and the twins are all asleep, but I'm going to put the baby monitor next to your bed in case she wakes up.

She shouldn't, though, because she's not having a bottle in the night any more.

'Whatever happens I'll be back in time to get everyone off to school. Any problems – give me a ring, or if you can't get through to me then try Vicky.'

'OK,' she said, rubbing her eyes. 'I hope she's all right.'

'Me too,' I told her. 'The ambulance will hopefully be here soon.'

I dashed into my bedroom, took my dressing gown off and grabbed a pair of jeans and a jumper that were lying on a chair and quickly put them on over my nightie. I could hear Hailey moaning in pain as I ran back down the stairs. She was curled up in a ball on the hall floor, whimpering like a wounded animal. She was in too much of a state for me to ask her any questions.

'Hailey, I'm here,' I told her, holding her hand. 'Hold on. The ambulance will be here soon. You're going to be OK.'

I kept on talking to her as I was worried she was going to lose consciousness. As I stroked her hair, I realised it was matted with blood.

What on earth had that sadistic monster done to her? I was incandescent with rage.

I could have cried with relief a few minutes later when I saw the glow of the ambulance's flashing lights through the front door. To my relief they didn't have their sirens going as I'd been worried they'd wake the girls as well as the rest of the street. I pulled on some boots and ran out to meet them. Two paramedics jumped out – a man and a woman.

'She's lying in the hall,' I babbled. 'She's been assaulted.'

'Do you know who did this to her?' asked the woman.

'She told me it was her partner,' I said. 'There's a history of domestic violence there. She's bleeding and in a lot of pain. He's really laid into her.'

'What's her name?' asked the woman.

'Hailey,' I said. 'I'm actually her daughter's foster carer. She doesn't live with me but somehow she managed to get herself here. I found her on the front doorstep and I'm not sure how long she'd been there. I didn't hear her at first.

'There's blood on her head. There's blood everywhere and she's absolutely freezing.'

'Don't worry,' the woman told me, placing a reassuring hand my arm. 'We'll get her to A&E as quick as we can.'

They got a stretcher from the back of the ambulance and ran into the hallway.

'Hi, Hailey. I'm Neil, a paramedic. We're going to take you to hospital now,' he told her, his voice kind and authoritative.

'I'm going to put a neck brace on you just as a precaution because we don't know until we get to hospital what your injuries are, and we need to keep you as still as possible.'

Hailey closed her eyes and nodded.

I felt helpless as I stood in the doorway and watched as they got to work. She moaned and cried out in pain as they gently lifted her onto the stretcher. They covered her with a foil blanket and fastened the straps over the top to secure her.

'Maggie,' she mumbled. 'Where's Maggie?'

'I'm here, Hailey,' I said, squeezing her hand gently.

'I'd like to go with her if I can?' I asked the female paramedic.

'Yes, that's fine,' she replied.

I grabbed my keys, mobile and handbag and followed them out of the door into the back of the ambulance.

'Hailey, your breathing's a little bit erratic so I'm going to give you some oxygen,' the female paramedic told her as she put a mask over her face.

As we sped through the traffic, sirens blaring, a million thoughts raced through my mind.

Please let her be OK, I prayed. *Please make Martin pay for this*.

Ten minutes later we pulled up to the hospital and Hailey was lifted out and wheeled into Accident and Emergency. I followed behind her.

'We're going to take her into a cubicle to be assessed. You can wait in one of the visitors' rooms,' a doctor told me. 'Someone will come and update you when we've got a clearer idea of what her injuries are.'

'No problem,' I replied. 'I just need to pop outside and make a quick phone call.'

I knew I had to ring Social Services and update them. I explained what had happened to the duty overnight social worker.

'Poor woman,' she sighed. 'Thanks for letting us know. I'll get Claire to call you first thing.'

'Thank you,' I replied. 'I'm going to stay with her at the hospital for as long as I can.'

My heart ached for Hailey. She didn't have anyone else to be there with her and hold her hand. I couldn't leave her on her own, although I knew I needed to be back to get the twins to school eventually.

I got a cup of horrible grainy coffee from the vending machine and went into one of the family rooms to wait. The chairs were hard and uncomfortable, so I paced up and down instead.

I couldn't stop thinking about how bad Hailey's injuries looked. She must have been in absolute agony. God only knew how she had managed to get herself to my doorstep. I was just glad that she trusted me and felt able to come to me for help.

I'd been waiting for fifteen minutes or so when a young doctor came walking towards me, a serious look on his face. He barely seemed old enough to be a doctor but he had a calm manner and seemed to know what he was doing.

'Are you with Hailey?' he asked. 'She wasn't able to tell us her surname.'

'It's Henley,' I said. 'Hailey Henley.'

'And do you know her date of birth?' he replied.

'I'm sorry, I don't,' I said. 'But I think she's 23.'

'Are you a relative?' he asked, looking confused.

'I'm a foster carer,' I said. 'I'm looking after Hailey's daughter. I don't think she has any family locally so she came to me for help.'

'As you know, she's been the victim of a very nasty assault,' he said gravely. 'She's got a broken nose, lots of bruising, possibly some broken ribs and a cut to the head.

'We'll need to do some X-rays and scans to check for internal bleeding and fractures, but we're getting her comfortable first and giving her some pain relief,' he continued. 'Her breathing's stabilized and her temperature is slowly increasing.'

'Thank God,' I sighed. 'Can I see her?'

He nodded.

'I'll take you through now. The other thing I need to ask is if you know who attacked her.'

'I'm pretty sure it was her husband,' I breathed out a heavy sigh. 'She's told me that he's hurt her in the past.'

143

'Because of the severity of her injuries we will need to ring the police,' the doctor told me. 'They'll want to come and speak to Hailey when she's feeling a bit stronger, and then she will have to decide whether she wants to co-operate with them and press charges.'

I'm glad the police weren't already on their way as I knew Hailey wasn't in any fit state to answer questions now.

'She was getting quite panicky and distressed so we've given her a bit of sedative to calm her down,' he told me.

I followed him down the corridor and he drew the curtain back to one of the cubicles. Hailey was lying on the bed, her eyes closed. Seeing her again it hit me how terrible she looked. Every part of her was literally black and blue.

'We've left the neck collar on just as a precaution before we scan her,' the doctor said, his face grim. 'I'll leave you two alone and will come to check on her in a bit.'

I wheeled up a stool next to Hailey and sat down.

'Hailey, it's Maggie,' I said gently, holding her hand. 'Can you hear me?'

Her eyes flickered and she nodded.

'The doctors are looking after you,' I soothed. 'You're safe now and you're going to be OK.'

She was too weak to talk. All I could do was hold her hand and try and reassure her. Ten minutes later a couple of nurses came in to take her to be X-rayed.

Then it was more waiting. It was 3 a.m. by now and I hoped everything was still quiet at home. Eventually Hailey was wheeled back into the cubicle and I held her hand while a nurse glued her head injury and cleaned her up. She was less groggy now and she winced in pain as her nose was bathed and taped up.

She was still very weak and in a lot of pain so I didn't want to encourage her to talk.

An hour or so later a doctor came back to see her.

'Hailey, your X-ray and scan results are back,' he said. 'You've got a couple of broken ribs and some internal bleeding.

'We're going to keep an eye on it and hope it will resolve itself without you needing an operation. A team is going to take you down to the ward now and try and get you comfortable. Is that OK?'

Hailey nodded.

It was a relief to hear that her injuries were treatable.

As I followed Hailey's trolley out of the cubicle, the doctor pulled me to one side.

'Her X-rays also showed some old injuries that are still healing,' he told me. 'There were another couple of fractured ribs and also she has a broken collarbone.'

'That's awful,' I sighed, 'but it doesn't surprise me. She's recently told me and the social worker about the level of violence she's had to live with on a daily basis.'

My heart ached for her. With injuries like that, she must have been in constant agony.

Hailey was still quite groggy, but as the pain relief kicked in she began to talk.

'He said he wanted us to run away,' she croaked. 'He wanted us to leave Jasmine and go away and live somewhere else and have another baby.

'He said Social Services wouldn't be able to do anything if we just upped and left and they wouldn't bother us any more.'

'What did you say?' I asked her.

'Something snapped inside me,' she continued, her voice as hoarse as sandpaper. 'I didn't want him to tell me what to do any more.

'He wasn't going to make me run away with him. Of course Social Services would find us. So I told him – I said to him I didn't want another baby, I wanted *my* baby. I wanted Jasmine.'

'What did he say?' I urged her to continue.

'He was so, so angry,' she replied, tears spilling out of her swollen eyes. 'He couldn't believe I had spoken out of turn to him like that.

'Then he just started laying into me. He was kicking and punching me. I rolled up on the floor to protect myself but he still carried on.'

'Oh, Hailey,' I said.

'In the end I played dead, Maggie. I lay there until I was sure he had gone to bed and was asleep.

'I was in so much pain but I used every bit of strength that I'd got to get myself up off the floor. I took some money from his wallet and crept out. I was so scared he was going to wake up and stop me.

'Everything hurt and I could hardly breathe but I knew if I could get to your house then I would be safe. I knew that you could help me.

'I managed to flag down a taxi. I don't know your address but I know the way there from when I come and see Jasmine.'

'Hailey, my love, you did the right thing. You're safe now.'

I sat with her until just after 5 a.m when I knew I had to head back.

'Hailey, I'm really sorry but I've got to leave now,' I told her. 'Jasmine will be waking up soon and I've got to get the girls ready for school. But I'm sure Claire will be coming to see you in a few hours when she finds out what's happened.'

'Please will you come back, Maggie?' she pleaded. 'And can you bring Jasmine? I want to see her.'

I could see the tears in her eyes.

'I'll have a chat to Claire and run it past her,' I replied. 'You take care of yourself. Try and get some rest and let the pain relief do its job.'

I rang a taxi to come and pick me up and walked out of the harshly lit hospital into the December morning. It was still pitch black outside and frost glittered on the car windscreens. After the heat and stuffiness of the ward, it was nice to feel the shock of the cold air on my face.

When I got back to the house all was still quiet. I knew there was no point in trying to get any sleep now as Jasmine normally woke up just after 6 a.m.

I went into the kitchen and flicked the kettle on. Once I'd made myself a steaming mug of tea, I flopped down on a chair at the kitchen table and put my head in my hands. Adrenalin had kept me going for the past few hours but now I was empty. I was totally and utterly exhausted.

I sat there in a daze, lost in my own thoughts until I heard Jasmine crying. I walked up the stairs to get her just as Louisa was coming out of her bedroom.

'Oh, you're here,' she said.

'You go back to bed and get some more sleep,' I told her. 'I'll sort out the baby.'

When I went in, Jasmine gave me a big smile. I picked her up and gave her a cuddle. She felt all warm and snuggly in my arms and I really needed that comfort after everything that had happened.

I took her downstairs and warmed up her bottle. As she gulped it down, she looked up at me with her big, trusting eyes.

'Poor Mummy,' I sighed. 'But I think she's going to be OK.'

Despite her horrific injuries, at least Hailey was in a safe place now. I hoped this would be a turning point for her. I hoped that she would finally realise that enough was enough.

Soon I heard the twins clattering about upstairs and Louisa brought them down. I felt I owed it to Louisa to be honest with her about what had happened, especially as she had held the fort for me at home in the middle of the night. She was old enough and mature enough to keep anything I told her confidential.

'How is Hailey?' she asked.

'She was in a bad way but hopefully she's going to be OK,' I replied.

'What happened?' Louisa's face was etched with concern.

'Unfortunately it looks like Jasmine's dad attacked her.'

'Oh no,' she gasped. 'That's terrible.'

'It is,' I replied. 'And sadly it's something that she's been living with for a long time.'

I knew it was going to be a long and rocky road ahead for Hailey. Physical injuries heal over time, but it is the mental scars that are often harder to bear.

A dramatic night turned into an ordinary morning. As the twins tucked into their toast and I fed Jasmine her porridge, I stared outside into the garden as the sun rose. It was the start of a new day and I honestly had no idea what it was going to bring.

THIRTEEN

Repercussions

I'd just got back from dropping the twins off at school when my mobile rang. It was Claire.

'Maggie, I've just heard what happened last night with Hailey,' she said breathlessly. 'Oh my God, is she all right? I'm getting in my car about to head to the hospital now.'

'It was horrendous, Claire,' I sighed. 'He'd beaten her to a pulp. I left her at 5 a.m. and she was still very shaken up and in a lot of pain, but the doctors were keeping a close eye on her.'

'Oh, the poor girl,' sighed Claire.

I explained what Hailey had told me about Martin's plan to leave the area and have another baby.

'What on earth was he thinking?' she exclaimed. 'Does he just think he can up and leave and have another baby without any repercussions? And what about Jasmine? Unbelievable.'

'I'd really like to go and see her again later today,' I told her. 'She was also desperate for me to bring Jasmine, but I said I would need to check with you. Would it be OK to take her in for a quick visit?'

'I don't see why not, in theory,' said Claire. 'But there is one thing that's bothering me. Do we know where Martin is?'

'Nope,' I replied. 'I was so caught up in getting Hailey to the hospital he was the last person on my mind. She told me that he was in bed when she snuck out last night. As far as I know the police are going up to the hospital to interview Hailey this morning now she's a bit more stable.'

'I'll have a chat to them when they get there,' Claire said. 'My other concern is whether Martin might come up to the hospital and try and find Hailey. Do you think there's any chance that he might? I couldn't risk having Jasmine there if that was the case.'

'Well, it is the local hospital, but Martin doesn't know that Hailey's been taken there. She's also on a ward now, so hopefully that will be more secure.'

'OK,' said Claire, sounding reassured. 'Let me go up to the hospital to see how Hailey is and give you a ring back.'

After putting down the phone to Claire, I gave my fostering agency a call. What had happened last night hadn't involved Jasmine but it affected her care and I wanted to keep them updated. I explained everything to Becky.

'Blimey, Maggie,' she sighed. 'That must have been horrendous. Poor woman, and how scary for you having her turn up on your doorstep in the middle of the night.'

'I didn't really think about it at the time,' I said. 'I just wanted to help her. She was in such a bad way, Becky.'

'How are *you* doing?' she asked.

The truth was I'd been so caught up in getting Hailey to the hospital, and then rushing back to make sure the kids were OK and getting them off to school, that I hadn't had a chance to register how I was feeling.

'I'm shattered,' I replied. 'But I'll make sure I get an early night tonight.'

'Make sure you look after yourself,' she told me. 'Could Vicky have the baby for you for a few hours this morning just so you can have a nap?'

'Honestly, I'll be OK,' I said. 'I want to try and get my notes typed up while everything is still fresh in my mind. But when Jasmine goes down for her sleep after lunch I might try and have a rest too.'

'Make sure you do that,' replied Becky. I appreciated the sentiment.

By the time I got home I was flagging a bit, but I was determined to get my recordings done. I'd only typed a couple of paragraphs when Claire called again.

'Oh, Maggie, you were right about Hailey,' she sighed. 'She's in a terrible state. I couldn't believe it when I saw her.'

'How does she seem in herself?' I asked.

'A little bit brighter. Her pain's under control but she's still very sore and she's desperate to see Jasmine.'

'What do you think?' I asked. 'Can I bring her up?'

'I don't think that would be a problem,' she replied. 'The ward seems very secure and the ward sister said you could bring her in outside the usual visiting times.'

Claire explained that she had also phoned the police. The hospital had already called them and they were sending a couple of officers to interview Hailey.

'They have a record of Martin from when we asked them to help us remove Jasmine,' she said.

'Hailey has also asked if you could sit with her when the police come to interview her. I think she needs some moral support.

'I offered but she was insistent it was you. She's very vulnerable and still very weak so I think it would be good if one of us was with her.'

'Yes, of course,' I said. 'That's fine. But I'll have Jasmine with me if I bring her up to the hospital.'

'I can look after her,' said Claire. 'I'll take her for a walk around.'

'Thanks,' I said. 'So when do you need me to come?'

'I'm sorry for the short notice, Maggie, but the police are apparently on their way now,' she said.

Right, that meant no time for any napping. On the way to the hospital I popped into the supermarket. I knew Hailey had absolutely nothing with her, and the pyjamas she'd been wearing were covered in blood. So I grabbed a nightie, a pack of knickers, a dressing gown and a few basic toiletries such as deodorant, a toothbrush and toothpaste. She was unlikely to be going anywhere for a few days and I wanted her to feel clean and comfortable and not be forced to wear a scratchy hospital gown.

I parked at the hospital and got Jasmine out of the car. Her eyes were as wide as saucers and she was moving her little head and looking all around her as we walked through the corridors and into the ward where Hailey was.

'We've come to see your mummy,' I told her, as I pushed back the curtain around Hailey's bed.

But Hailey didn't look very much like the mummy she knew. Her face was still very swollen and covered in bruises and she had a big gauze bandage over her nose. Claire was sitting beside her.

'Look who I've brought to see you,' I smiled, trying to mask the shock I felt inside. Even though I'd only left her a few hours previously, I still couldn't get used to the state she was in.

Her face lit up and she held out her arms. Jasmine stared at her, unsure, and clung onto me.

'She doesn't know me,' sobbed Hailey. 'She's scared of me.'

'Just talk to her,' I said, trying to reassure her. 'She'll soon recognise your voice.'

'Hello sweetheart,' she sniffled. 'Mummy's missed you. Can I have a cuddle?'

I gently handed Jasmine over to her, willing the baby not to cry. To my relief she didn't.

'Is that too uncomfortable for you with your ribs?' I asked Hailey.

'No, it's fine,' she said. 'It's worth any pain.'

She held on tightly to her daughter, nuzzling into her neck, and I could see how much she was relishing that cuddle.

'Mummy's here,' she told her gently, stroking the back of her head. 'I'm going to fight for you, my baby.'

Just then a nurse popped her head around the curtains.

'I'm sorry to interrupt but the police are here to see you, Hailey.'

Hailey looked terrified as two officers came in. I knew this was going to be incredibly difficult and traumatic for her to talk about, so I was pleased to see one of them was a young woman who looked a similar age to Hailey. The other officer was a man in his forties who had a kind face.

'Hello Mrs Henley, is now a good time to have a chat?' he asked.

'I don't think there's ever going to be a good time but I know I have to do it,' she sighed. She sounded the most decisive that I'd ever heard her.

'I want Maggie to be here,' she said, suddenly frightened again.

'Of course,' I told her, squeezing her hand. 'I'm happy to stay.'

'I'll take Jasmine off and give you all time to talk,' said Claire, gently lifting her out of Hailey's arms. 'I'll bring her back in a little while.'

Hailey's eyes didn't leave Jasmine as Claire carried her out of the ward. While the officers introduced themselves to Hailey I poured her a glass of water from the jug next to her bed.

'We know you've been through a lot in the past 24 hours and the doctors have told us you have sustained some serious injuries,' the male officer told us. 'So we're going to take a brief statement today, but when you feel a bit stronger and you're out of hospital we'd like to do a longer interview so we can go through things in more detail. Does that sound OK?'

Hailey nodded. I could see she was trembling and I put my hand on her arm to try and reassure her.

'Can you tell us in your own words what happened to you last night?' the female officer asked. 'I know it must be very traumatic for you so if you need a break then let us know.'

Hailey started to cry, silent tears leaving track marks over her bruised and battered face.

'Take your time,' I soothed, handing her a glass of water.

With shaking hands, Hailey took a sip then she began to talk.

In between gulping sobs, she told them exactly what she had told me – how Martin had wanted them to run away, leave Jasmine with me and have another baby.

'But I didn't want to,' she pleaded. 'I told him I could never leave Jasmine.'

She paused.

'That's when he lost it and started hitting me.'

'Hailey, I know it's upsetting, but we need you to tell us exactly how he hurt you,' the female officer said gently while her colleague took notes.

Even though Hailey had already told me a little bit of what had happened, it was horrendous to hear her describing how Martin had subjected her to such a horrific attack, kicking and punching her until she had collapsed on the floor.

'He punched me straight in the face,' she said. 'I was so shocked I staggered backwards. Then he did it again.

'I heard my nose crack and it felt like it was going to explode. I could taste blood in my mouth and it was pouring down onto my clothes.

'I fell onto the floor and that's when he started kicking me like a football. He booted me in the head and my ears started ringing.

'At first I think I was screaming, but then I was in too much pain. I just lay there and took it. I think I just gave up. I honestly thought I was going to die.'

All I could do was hold her hand as she sobbed. 'You're doing so well,' I told her. 'You're so, so brave.'

'The doctors have told us that your scans and X-rays showed up some older injuries,' the officer said. 'Has your husband hurt you before?'

Hailey looked down, ashamed.

'All the time,' she nodded. 'It's become a normal part of my life.

'He hurt me so many times but I didn't dare go to the doctor or the hospital because I knew they'd ask how it happened. If

I made an appointment like that he'd insist on coming with me in case I told them the truth.

'So I just got used to being in constant pain.'

I couldn't imagine how she had lived like that for so long.

'Hailey, what we need to ask you now is extremely important,' said the male officer. 'We need to know if you want to press charges against your husband for assaulting you.

'What I would say is that I feel we'd have a good chance of a conviction as we've got medical reports and we will shortly take photographs of your injuries.

'But it's important for you to know that if your husband pleads not guilty, then there will be a trial, and it's highly likely that at that trial you will be called to give evidence against him.'

Hailey's face fell.

'What, I'd have to stand up in court in front of him, in front of everyone and tell them what he'd done to me?'

The officer nodded.

'If that did happen you'd have lots of support from the police and from Social Services,' the female officer told her. 'We'd hold your hand throughout the whole process.'

'Could he be sent to prison?' she asked.

'There are no guarantees, but for a serious assault like this then I would think a custodial sentence is likely,' the man told her.

I knew this would be a terrifying prospect for Hailey and there was nothing I could do to influence her decision.

'I want to,' she said firmly. 'I want to press charges. I don't want him to hurt me any more and I want him to pay for what he's done to me.'

She sounded very definite and decisive, so different from the meek and scared woman I'd seen up until now. I was so proud of her.

'What happens now?' she asked.

'What we'd like to do is take some photographs of your injuries,' he told her. 'Then, when we leave here, we'll go and bring your husband in for questioning.

'Depending on the outcome of those interviews, then we will decide if we have enough evidence to charge him with assault.'

'Can you let me know what happens?' she asked.

'Of course,' the female officer replied. 'We'll stay in touch through your social worker as I know you haven't got a mobile.'

'Thank you,' Hailey smiled meekly.

I went to the loo while the female officer took a few brief photos of Hailey's injuries. When I came back, they'd gone.

'You did so well to get through that,' I told her, squeezing her hand. 'You're so strong, Hailey.'

'I don't feel very strong,' she said, tears pricking her eyes again. 'I should have left him a long time ago but I was so frightened, Maggie. I still am.

'The stupid thing is I'd already made my decision last week. I'd decided to leave him and fight for Jasmine.

'I could kick myself. I should have said something to you or Claire and left him then. Then this would never have happened.

'I'd had enough,' she said. 'Now I know more than ever if I stayed with Martin he would kill me. What good is that for Jasmine?

'I'm going to fight for my daughter. I'm going to show Social Services I can do it on my own.'

'Good for you,' I said, and meant every word.

Claire came back with Jasmine and we told her what Hailey had decided.

'I'm going to have an emergency meeting with my manager and Neil, the IRO, this afternoon to decide how best to proceed,' she told us. 'After everything that has happened with Martin, I think it's safe to say that as of now your joint parental assessment will be cancelled.

'Then, when you're feeling a bit better, we need to have a chat about finding you a safe place to go, Hailey, and also starting your own individual assessment.'

Hailey nodded.

'But the main thing is for you to focus on getting better,' Claire smiled.

'I'm going to go now and let you get some rest,' I told Hailey.

I could see Jasmine was getting hungry as well as sleepy so I needed to go home and get her some lunch. 'If it's OK with Claire then I'll bring Jasmine back in to see you tomorrow.'

'That should be fine, Maggie,' she nodded. 'Maggie, I'll walk out to the car park with you.'

As we wandered out through the hospital we talked about the events that had unfolded.

'I'm so pleased that Hailey's decided to leave him,' I said.

'I am too, but I'm being cautious about it,' said Claire. 'You and I both know that domestic violence cases are often not as simple and straightforward as that.

'Hailey's willing to prosecute now and wants to fight for her baby, but will that be the case four months down the line?'

Sadly, I knew from experience that she was right. When someone is in pain or shock they will often say one thing, but once they've had time to think about the implications and what it really means, they often change their mind. I knew that could happen with Hailey right up until any court case that might happen. Her resolve would also depend on what pressure Martin put on her.

By the time I got home, I was delirious with tiredness. I couldn't wait for the day to end, and when the twins and Jasmine went to bed at 7.30 p.m., I wasn't far behind them.

As I crawled into bed, I couldn't help but think of Hailey in the hospital. I hoped she was doing OK and was comfortable and managing to get some sleep.

In the morning, after I'd taken the twins to school, I took Jasmine up to the hospital. Hailey was still very sore and bruised but she'd managed to eat some breakfast.

'It's really noisy in here but I got three or four hours sleep,' she said, through her swollen and cracked lips.

I'd been there an hour or so when a nurse popped her head in. 'Hailey, there's a police officer here to see you,' she said.

It was the female officer who had come to take a statement from her the previous day.

'How are you doing, Hailey?' she asked.

'All right,' Hailey replied. 'Why are you here? What's happened?'

'There's nothing to worry about,' the officer said gently. 'I just wanted to come and update you in person. We questioned your husband yesterday and we felt there was enough evidence to charge him with assault.'

Hailey sighed with relief.

'So is he locked up now?' she asked.

'He was kept in custody overnight but he was charged this morning and bailed.'

'What do you mean?' asked Hailey, looking stunned. 'You mean you let him go?'

The officer nodded, and my heart sank.

'The court decided to grant him bail, but one of the conditions of that is he's not allowed to approach you,' she said. 'If he does then he will be arrested.'

Hailey looked totally shocked.

'We will keep in touch with you but any problems at all then please give us a ring,' the officer told her before she left. 'You take care of yourself.'

'Maggie, I can't believe they let him out,' Hailey gasped as soon as we were alone again. 'What if he tries to find me?'

'Claire will have a chat to you later, but she's going to try and find you somewhere safe to go like a refuge. Martin won't be able to find you there.'

'But what if he comes here to the hospital?' she said. 'He knew I was badly hurt and he doesn't have to be a genius to work out where I am. There's only one main hospital in this area.'

I could see she was getting more and more hysterical.

'Hailey, I know you're scared but you need to calm down,' I told her, doing my best to sound in control. 'It's not going to do your health any good if you're getting worked up. If Martin was going to find you he'd have to walk up and down every ward and check every single bed.'

'I know him, Maggie, and he'd do it,' she said. 'He always said if I left him then he'd find me and kill me. He wouldn't care if he was arrested.'

Hailey was genuinely terrified of Martin and what he might do. I knew the police didn't have the resources to send someone to sit with her 24 hours a day.

'Let me go and talk to the nurses and see if there's anything they can do,' I told her.

I went to chat to the ward sister and explained the situation to her. She was very understanding.

'They've agreed to move you to a private room,' I told her. 'It's right at the end of the ward so Martin would have to walk through the entire ward to find you as well as going past the nurse's station.

'If someone came in the ward like that they could have security here in minutes. Does that make you feel any better?'

'Kind of,' she shrugged, though she didn't look very convinced. 'I just know what he's like, Maggie. He'd do whatever it took to track me down. I'm just so scared.'

She started to cry. I felt helpless, but I took her in my arms.

'I know you are,' I said. 'But it will be OK.'

I hoped beyond hope that I was speaking the truth.

FOURTEEN

Hunted Down

Over the next few days I took Jasmine up to the hospital every day to see her mother.

Physically, Hailey was getting stronger. Her bruises had turned every colour of the rainbow and were now beginning to fade and she wasn't in as much pain. But emotionally I could see she still had a long way to go. She was mentally exhausted and she was still living on her nerves, terrified that Martin would find her.

On the upside, I could see that in her head she had started to build a future for herself and Jasmine, and the thought of that was keeping her going. This was the longest that she'd ever been away from Martin since she was a teenager, and it had allowed her to imagine a life without him. When she held Jasmine she'd chat to her about all the things they would do together.

'I can't wait to take you to the park and push you on the swings,' she told her. 'And one day, when I have some money, I'll take you shopping and buy you a pretty dress.'

It was heartbreaking to hear her talk about these normal, everyday things, things that we all take for granted, but that she had never been allowed to do with her own daughter.

In the meantime, Claire was busy trying to find a place in a refuge for Hailey for when she was discharged. The doctors had said she would probably be well enough to leave in a couple of days and, of course, she couldn't go home.

I could see it was preying on Hailey's mind and Claire and I did our best to allay her fear.

'Where will the refuge be?' she asked.

'The reality is we might not be able to find a place for you in a local refuge,' Claire told her. 'So you need to be prepared for the fact it might be a little bit further afield.'

'I don't mind,' said Hailey. 'In a way I'd feel safer if it wasn't round here as Martin's less likely to find me.'

'Refuges are specially designed so people can't find you,' I reassured her. 'They're protected addresses so the only people that know where they are are the police and Social Services.

'Everyone who stays there has to sign a contract to say they won't disclose the address to anyone. Even their family and friends don't know it.'

'What if I do have to go to one further way,' she asked. 'I'll still be able to see Jasmine, though, won't I?'

'Yes, of course,' said Claire. 'We'll make sure of that.'

We tried to answer all her questions.

'Where will I sleep?' she asked. 'Will I have to share a room?'

'Each refuge is different,' Claire replied. 'But you'll definitely have your own room, and then there will probably be communal areas where you can cook and eat and do your washing.

'Don't worry,' she continued, 'when the time comes, I'll take you there and we'll get you settled. You don't have to do this on your own, Hailey.'

Often people assume that when someone leaves an abusive relationship they must feel euphoric, like a weight has been lifted. In my experience, that was true for some women but for others, like Hailey, the future could feel terrifying and overwhelming.

'What about clothes and things?' she said. 'I haven't got anything apart from the bits Maggie bought me. And I don't have any money. Martin did all that – I was never allowed any money of my own. I don't even have a bank account.'

'Don't worry, that can all be sorted out when you're at the refuge,' I told her.

Clothes were easy to sort out. 'I've got a couple of friends who are a similar size to you who are always giving me things,' I continued. 'I've got a huge bag in the loft that I can sort through.'

I made a mental note to ask Vicky as she was as petite as Hailey and might have a few spare things.

'And all the staff are usually women and you'll get so much support there,' added Claire. 'They can help you sort out benefits and register with a doctor, as well as offering you therapy and counselling. There'll be lots of other women there who have been through similar things to you.'

One thing that Hailey was very determined about was that she was going to get Jasmine back.

'So when can I start my parenting assessment?' she asked Claire.

'There's no rush,' Claire replied. 'When you're feeling better and you're out of hospital then we can start to look at how we're going to do it. A lot of what you've done previously can also be taken into consideration – like how you've been with Jasmine at Maggie's house.'

'But not at the contact centre,' Hailey insisted. 'I was a different person when I was with him. I didn't even dare pick Jasmine up without his permission. I just kept my head down in those sessions so he had nothing to get angry with me about.'

'Well, this time you can be assessed all by yourself with no one breathing down your neck,' I reassured her. 'You're free to be the kind of mother to Jasmine you want to be.'

Before the new parenting assessment could start, Claire needed to tell Martin that the old one had been cancelled. But first she needed to bring Hailey up to speed.

'Hailey, I need to talk to you about Martin,' Claire told her one morning when we both came up to the hospital.

Hailey's face fell and she looked terrified.

'Why, what is it?' she gasped, clinging on to Jasmine. 'What's happened? Has he been here? Is he trying to find me?'

'It's nothing at all for you to worry about,' said Claire. 'I just wanted to let you know that I've asked him to come to a meeting at Social Services with me and Neil, the IRO.'

'What for?' she asked, her eyes still wide with fear.

'We need to explain to him that because of everything that has happened and with him being charged with assault, we're going to have to cancel the parental assessment.'

'But will he still be allowed to see Jasmine?' Hailey asked, looking panicked. She clutched the baby even tighter to her chest.

'No, all contact has been suspended, too,' said Claire.

'But what if he asks where I am?' she said.

'I'll just tell him that I can't disclose that information and that's all I can say.'

'He's going to go mental,' Hailey sighed. 'He won't take no for an answer.'

'Well, if that happens we will deal with it,' Claire replied, reassuringly.

I completely understood Hailey's concerns. Martin wasn't the kind of person who would take this sort of news lying down. But the fact was, he had to. He didn't have a leg to stand on after being charged with such a serious offence as assault.

That morning I headed home on a mission to sort some things out for Hailey. While Jasmine went down for her nap I got some bags of clothes down from the loft.

As I was going through them, Louisa came back.

'What are you doing home so early?' I asked her.

'Charlie said he'd take me shopping for my Christmas present, so I took a half day.'

'Blimey, he's organised,' I said. 'It's only December the eighth!'

'Well, he wants it to be special,' she smiled. 'Anyway, what are you doing?'

'I'm sorting some clothes out for Hailey.'

'Oh, how is she?' asked Louisa.

'OK,' I replied. 'Hopefully she's moving to a refuge next week, so I'm trying to get some bits and pieces together for her as she left with absolutely nothing. I had these in the loft and hopefully Vicky can give me some stuff.'

'I can sort some bits out for you if you want,' Louisa offered.

'That would be great, lovey,' I said, beaming at her. 'I think you're probably a similar size to Hailey.'

'And my stuff will be way cooler than Vicky's,' she laughed. 'The poor girl doesn't want to wear hand-me-downs from a forty-something!'

'Oi, don't be so cheeky – you mind your elders,' I chuckled. 'Thanks sweetheart, that would be brilliant.'

With Hailey's wardrobe pretty much sorted I started to worry about more important things, like Martin's meeting at Social Services. The following day I was on tenterhooks as I waited for Claire to call and let me know how it had gone.

When my phone rang just after lunch, I pounced on it.

'Hi, Maggie, it's Helen,' said a voice.

'Helen?' I asked, completely confused.

'Polly and Daisy's adoption worker.'

'Oh, Helen, I'm sorry, I was miles away,'

She explained that she was ringing to sort out a date when the twins' potential adopters could come round and meet me.

'We're hoping that they'll manage to get to panel before Christmas but that's still a couple of weeks away,' she said.

'So, in the meantime, they'd like to meet you and hear more about the girls.'

'Of course,' I replied. 'It's important that they know as much as possible.'

We set up a date for Lizzie and Joe to come round the following week.

As I came off the phone, my head was spinning as I tried to absorb everything that was happening. I was trying to make sure that Hailey and Jasmine were OK at the same time as juggling the twins' impending adoption. I felt my blood pressure rise at the thought of it.

Claire phoned half an hour later.

'How did it go with Martin?' I asked.

'I was very matter-of-fact,' said Claire. 'I told him that the parental assessment had ended because he had been charged with such a serious offence, and that my recommendation was that he didn't have contact with Jasmine at this point in time.'

'How did he take that?' I asked.

'He was surprisingly OK at first,' she replied. 'He was still doing his Mr Charming act and implying it was all a terrible misunderstanding.

'But then he started asking about Hailey and that's when his facade slipped. He kept on asking me where she was, but I said I wasn't at liberty to give out that information. I told him all I could tell him was that Hailey was safe but that she was choosing not to come home at this point in time.

'That's when he lost it,' she sighed. 'In the end he was kicking off so much we had to call security to remove him from the building.'

'Well, at least he knows,' I said, 'although Hailey is going be even more nervous and jumpy when you tell her how it went. The sooner she can move to a refuge the better.'

'The good news is that I think I've found her a space in one about a twenty-five-minute drive from you,' replied Claire. 'I'll be able to confirm later this afternoon and then she should be able to move there on Monday.'

'That's brilliant,' I said, relief flooding through me.

The following day was Saturday, so I took the twins and Jasmine round to Vicky's to collect some clothes for Hailey. She handed me two huge bags full.

'Thank you,' I told her. 'You're so generous.'

'To be honest I've been needing to have a clear-out for ages – or a wardrobe detox, as posh people like to call it,' she laughed.

'Have you got time for a cup of tea?'

'I'm sorry, but I've got to dash off,' I said. 'I promised I'd take the twins swimming this morning.'

The pool was over the other side of the city and to get there we had to drive through the centre of town. The traffic was terrible and every single traffic light seemed to be against us. I stopped at a pedestrian crossing on the high street and waited for the hordes of shoppers to cross. I was lost in my own thoughts until out of the corner of my eye I caught sight of a man walking across the road in front of me. There was something familiar about his fair hair and the coat he was wearing.

Just as I'd registered him, he turned, saw me staring at him and did a double take. For a millisecond our eyes locked and I saw a flicker of recognition in his face.

Martin.

My heart thumped out of my chest as he came marching towards my car.

Oh God, Jasmine was in the back. What if he tried to grab her?

I quickly flicked the central locking on. Fortunately my rear windows were tinted so it was hard to see inside them.

He came round to my side of the car and started pounding on the window.

'Where is she?' he yelled. 'Where's my wife? Tell me where my wife is, you bitch!'

His face was contorted in anger and I could see the rage in his wide eyes as he hammered on the glass.

'Hailey, are you in there?' he shouted. 'I need to talk to you.'

I was panic-stricken. I could see people staring at us, looking over.

Please change, lights, I told myself. *Please change.*

'Why is that funny man shouting at you?' asked Polly innocently, from the back. Thankfully the girls weren't fazed at all.

'I think he's cross about something,' I said, as breezily as I could.

Mercifully the lights changed a few seconds later. I've never been so relieved to see a green traffic light. As I sped away from Martin I could see him shouting and gesticulating at me in the distance. Other cars were beeping at him as he was still standing in the middle of the street.

I'd driven a few minutes down the road when I realised my hands were shaking. I pulled over into a side street and parked.

I was relieved to see that Jasmine was fast asleep in the back, oblivious to what had just happened, and the twins seemed fine too.

'I'm glad the silly man has gone,' said Polly.

'Me too, sweetie,' I sighed. 'Me too.'

'Can we go swimming now?' asked Daisy.

'I'm really sorry girls but I'm feeling a bit poorly so I think we need to go home,' I told her. 'I promise I'll take you another time.'

I could tell the twins were disappointed but I needed to be in the safety of my own four walls.

I took a few deep breaths to compose myself, then I fumbled in my bag for my mobile and called Claire.

'You'll never believe what's just happened,' I said. 'I saw Martin.'

She could obviously hear how shaken I was.

'Get yourself home, Maggie, and I'll be there in ten minutes,' she said.

All the way back I was looking in my rear-view mirror, half expecting to see Martin behind me. In reality, I knew he was on foot so it was highly unlikely, but I was really shaken up.

Claire pulled up outside the house just as I did.

'You get the girls in and I'll go and make us a cup of tea,' she said.

I sat down at the kitchen table, took a deep breath and started to explain to Claire what had happened.

'I can't believe it,' I sighed, taking a deep gulp of warming tea. 'I can't believe I just randomly bumped into him like that.'

'What an awful coincidence,' she said. 'You must have been really scared.

'I've seen him when he's angry and he's a nasty piece of work.'

'Obviously log it in your notes, as the twins' social worker will need to know,' said Claire. 'Are you going to report it to the police?'

'I don't think so,' I sighed. 'It was in a public place and we saw each other completely by chance.

'He wasn't trespassing or anything, it was just a completely random thing.'

My mind quickly turned to Hailey. 'Should we tell Hailey?' I said.

'I don't think it's worth it,' said Claire. 'It will make her even more anxious and nervous.'

I knew she was right. Hailey would never believe it was just a terrible coincidence. She'd think Martin was stalking me. I took comfort in the fact that as a foster carer my address was protected. It wasn't on any databases or in any phone books, and solicitors and parents were never given it. It would be very difficult for him to track me down.

To my relief, the rest of the weekend passed without incident. After the stress of what had happened with Martin, the girls and I had a very quiet couple of days in the house. On Sunday evening, I was just locking up downstairs before heading to bed for an early night when my mobile rang.

I saw Vicky's number flash up.

'You're ringing late,' I said, when I answered. 'Is everything OK?'

'Maggie, there's a bit of a situation going on here,' she told me, her voice breathless with panic.

'What is it?' I asked. 'Are you OK?'

'Maggie, is Jasmine's dad quite tall with fair hair?'

'Yes,' I said. 'But why are you asking me that?'

'Because I think he's outside my front door,' she told me. Then the line went dead.

FIFTEEN

A Safe Haven

'Vicky?' I yelled down the phone. 'Are you there? Tell me what's happening.'

But the line was definitely dead. All sorts of thoughts were racing through my mind as I paced up and down the kitchen in my dressing gown. What the hell was Martin doing at her house? How on earth had he found her? What did he want? I'd never forgive myself if anything happened to her or her foster children.

I tried calling her back several times but the line went straight to voicemail. I was really panicking now and I knew I couldn't wait any longer. What if Martin had got inside the house and attacked her? She could be lying injured on the floor just like poor Hailey had been.

I was about to dial 999 when my phone rang again. I pounced on it.

'Vicky,' I said. 'Tell me what's going on. Are you OK?'

'I'm so sorry, Maggie,' she said. 'He put a brick through my front window. I heard the crash and I didn't know what it was so I had to hang up.'

'Oh God,' I gasped. 'Have you called the police?'

'Yes,' she said. 'That was the first thing I did. They're on their way. I knew you'd be worrying, that's why I wanted to call you back.'

She paused, then added, 'I think they've just turned up, so I'll ring you back, OK?'

'OK,' I told her. 'Vicky, please be careful. Martin's a nasty piece of work.'

There was absolutely no chance of me going to bed now. Not until I knew Vicky and the kids were safe. I made myself a cup of tea and counted down the minutes until Vicky called me back. I was relieved when she rang twenty minutes later.

'The police have just gone and it's all calm again,' she said, sighing.

'Where's Martin?' I asked.

'They've arrested him for criminal damage and taken him off to the station for questioning.'

'He didn't hurt you or the kids, did he?' I asked.

'No, the kids are all in bed. Amazingly they slept through the whole thing. He didn't manage to get into the house. My living room is a mess and covered in glass, but we'll survive.'

I was enormously relieved that she was OK.

'I'm so, so sorry,' I said. 'How did you know it was him?'

Vicky explained that she'd been watching TV in the living room when she had heard someone pounding on her front door.

'It was a man's voice yelling, "Hailey, I know you and Jasmine are in there. I just want to talk to you." I didn't twig who it was at first. I thought it was some drunk on his way back from the pub who'd got confused.

'So I put the chain on and opened the door and told him he'd got the wrong house and there was no Hailey or Jasmine here.

'Then he accused me of lying and said he knew this was your house because he'd followed you back from Social Services one day and he knew you lived here. It was then that I recognised the names and realised it must be Jasmine's dad.

'He was very aggressive so I shut the door on him and called the police straight away before ringing you.'

I couldn't believe what I was hearing. I remembered the time months ago after the review meeting at Social Services when I'd seen Martin outside smoking. I'd felt uneasy and I had good reason. He must have followed me back to Vicky's when I'd gone to collect Jasmine, and then assumed it was my house.

'I'm just glad he followed you here and not to your place, otherwise things could be much worse,' said Vicky.

She was right. If Martin knew where I lived it would mean that Jasmine would have to be moved immediately to another carer.

'I'm so sorry you had to go through that, Vicky,' I sighed.

'It's OK,' she said. 'It was scary at the time. I was worried he was going to kick the front door in, but the police were here really quickly.'

'But what if he comes back when they release him?' I said. 'Doesn't that put you and your kids at risk?'

'Thankfully he doesn't realise that I know you,' she said. 'The police are aware of the situation so they're going to reiterate that nobody called Maggie lives at this address, that he got the wrong house and his wife isn't in the area.'

The whole incident had left me feeling really unsettled. As soon as I'd finished speaking to Vicky, I rang Social Services and left an urgent message with the duty social worker asking Claire to ring me. She called me straight back.

'I can't believe he had the audacity to turn up on your friend's doorstep!' Claire sounded very angry. 'He's not going to give up, is he?'

'The sooner Hailey gets to this refuge, the better,' I agreed.

Fortunately, she was being discharged from the hospital the following morning.

'I'll see you tomorrow,' said Claire. 'At least we know he's safely locked up at the police station overnight.'

I knew Hailey wouldn't truly rest until he was behind bars for the foreseeable future. I felt on edge too, after everything that had happened over the past few days. Everywhere I went I was looking over my shoulder – at the supermarket, when I was driving in the car, if there was a knock at the door. I was constantly on my guard.

I hardly slept a wink that night, worrying about Hailey and Jasmine and wondering where Martin was going to turn up next.

The following morning, as soon as I'd dropped the twins off at school, I headed to the refuge, where Claire would be bringing Hailey directly from the hospital. Hailey had asked me to be there for moral support, and she also wanted to see Jasmine and show her where she would be living.

I pulled up on the street outside the large Victorian detached house. It was unmarked, so no one passing by would realise it was a women's refuge. There was no sign of Claire and Hailey yet. Jasmine had fallen asleep in her car seat, so I waited until I saw Claire's car pull up further down the street.

As they walked towards me, I was struck by how frail Hailey seemed and how incredibly nervous she looked. She was wearing some jeans and a pink jumper I recognised as Louisa's, plus a puffer jacket of Vicky's, as well as some new trainers Claire had got her. It was nice to see her in something other than the shapeless threadbare clothes and men's shoes Martin had forced her to wear. For the first time she looked like a young woman.

She was carrying a Sainsbury's carrier bag and I could have kicked myself for not thinking to bring her a rucksack or a holdall to put her stuff from the hospital in.

'You finally escaped, then?' I smiled. 'How does it feel to be out of hospital?'

'A bit strange,' she mumbled.

'Is this it?' she asked, nervously gesturing to the house.

'It's a lovely old building,' said Claire. 'Lots of character. Shall we go in?'

I could see Hailey was very hesitant and she hung back with me, letting Claire take the lead.

Claire pressed the button on the intercom and I noticed that there were CCTV cameras above the front door.

'You see it's all very secure,' she told Hailey. 'They can monitor exactly who's coming in.'

'It's Claire Humphries from Social Services here to see the manager,' she said into the speaker.

Someone buzzed us in. We went through the large door into a small entrance area. There was a glass hatch and I could see an office with a couple of women behind it. One of them, a tall dark-haired woman in her forties, smiled at us and came to the hatch.

'Can I see your ID please?' she asked us.

Claire handed over her Social Services ID and my foster carer ID card.

'This is Hailey, who's coming to stay here,' she told them.

'Hello, love,' she said to her. 'Don't look so scared, we're a friendly bunch. I'll just buzz you through and the manager will be there to meet you in a few minutes.'

She pressed a button and another security door opened. We stepped into a large hallway which echoed with noise. The sound of children's TV blasted out from one of the rooms. I could hear women talking and laughing, and a baby crying upstairs. A couple of women walked past and smiled at us. Hailey chewed on her lip and looked terrified.

'It's going to be OK,' I said, giving her arm a reassuring squeeze, but she didn't look so sure.

Eventually a tall, grey-haired woman in jeans and a shirt came out to meet us. She had a kind, soft face.

'I'm Anna, the hostel manager,' she said, smiling at us.

'This is Hailey,' said Claire.

'I hear you've been in hospital,' Anna said, turning to Hailey, her face full of genuine concern. 'How are you feeling now?'

'Better,' mumbled Hailey, struggling to meet Anna's eyes. 'Still a bit wobbly.'

I could see she'd retreated back into her shell and had become the old quiet Hailey who was scared to make eye contact with anyone.

'Your key worker Liz is in a meeting at the minute but I'll introduce you later,' she told her. 'In the meantime I'll show you round.'

The exterior might have been grand but the interior of the house was basic, though clean.

'There are twenty rooms here,' she said. 'Some are singles and some are bigger family rooms for women who come here with their children.

'I'll show you the downstairs areas first before I take you up to your bedroom.'

She led us into a large communal kitchen with a long table and laundry area.

'You'll be allocated your own shelf and a cupboard where you can keep your food,' Anna told her.

'We have a rota so everyone takes it in turns to do jobs like sweeping up and wiping down after meals, and we expect everyone to do their own washing up.'

Then she took us into a huge living room with a sofa, beanbags and a TV, and off that was a playroom full of books and toys. None of it was plush and everything was well worn, but it was light and bright and it had a homely feel about it.

'Jasmine will like this,' said Hailey, picking up some of the baby toys out of a storage box.

'We run weekly mother-and-baby sessions in here,' said Anna.

'I'm sure Maggie and I can work things out so she brings Jasmine up for those,' Claire told Hailey.

'Oh, can you?' Hailey replied, her face lighting up. 'I'd like that.'

Afterwards Anna took us upstairs.

'This is your bedroom,' she said, unlocking a security door. It was a small room with a single bed and a chest of drawers and a cot in the corner. There was a harsh strip light on the ceiling but it was clean and it had cheerful purple walls.

'There's a shared bathroom and toilet down the hall which you can look at in your own time,' said Anna. 'I'll leave you to settle in. Then it would be great if you could come down to the office, as I need to run through a few procedures and health and safety stuff with you.'

As she left and closed the door, Hailey looked like she was going to cry. There was a tatty net curtain on the window but it wasn't thick enough to block out all the light.

'We can fasten a blanket up there as a temporary measure and then I'll get you a curtain and bring it in,' I told her. 'We can easily cheer this place up with a lamp, some plants and a few photos of Jasmine.'

Suddenly Hailey noticed the cot and her face lit up.

'There's a cot!' she said excitedly. 'Is Jasmine going to be moving in here with me?'

'No, Hailey, I'm afraid she's not,' Claire told her. 'Not just yet anyway. Remember how we talked about the fact that we have to do another parenting assessment with just you on your own? Once that's finished, then we can make a decision about whether Jasmine can come out of the care system and live with you.'

Hailey sat down on the bed and burst into tears. I could tell she was completely overwhelmed by everything.

'I'm so stupid,' she sobbed. 'I just want Jasmine to be here with me. I wish it more than anything.'

'Hailey, you're certainly not stupid,' said Claire gently. 'We're not saying that's never going to happen. It's something we can look towards for the future.'

Hailey seemed terrified by the whole thing.

'What if I hate it here?' she asked, drying her eyes with her sleeve. 'What if I don't want to stay?'

'It's going to be OK,' I told her, sitting next to her on the bed and taking her hand in mine. 'You'll soon get used to it and get to know people. The women downstairs seemed really friendly and Anna was very nice.'

'Will I have to talk to other people?' Hailey replied.

'Not if you don't want to,' Claire told her. 'But some women like the support being in a refuge gives them, and they find it really helpful talking to other people who have been through similar experiences.'

She added, 'Let's go down and meet your key worker and fill in the paperwork with the manager.'

Liz, the keyworker, was a smiley blonde woman, very gentle and welcoming.

'Don't look so worried,' she told Hailey. 'I'll introduce you to everyone later and we'll help you settle in.

'We're a small refuge so everyone knows each other and we all help each other out.'

She ran through some documents with Hailey that she had to sign, including a contract declaring that she would never disclose the refuge's address.

'This is probably the most important aspect of you being here,' Liz told her. 'The one condition we ask of every woman entering this refuge is that you can't tell anyone where you are.

'That doesn't just mean your ex-partner, it also includes friends, family, anyone. If you go against this, then you're not only jeopardising your safety but the safety of all the other women and children here, and you'll be asked to leave. We'll give you a PO box address which you can use if people want to contact you.'

Jasmine was still fast asleep, so I left her with Claire while I went to get the suitcase that I'd left in the car.

'Here's a few clothes to tide you over,' I told Hailey. 'And I'll start getting you some things together to make your bedroom more cosy.'

'Thank you, Maggie,' she said, giving me a weak smile.

'I hope the rest of the day goes OK and you manage to sleep tonight,' Claire told her. 'And Maggie and I will see you tomorrow morning. Any problems, then text me or give me a ring.'

Social Services had paid for Hailey to have a basic mobile so they and the police could contact her.

Hailey looked like a scared little girl as she watched us walk out of the front door. I could see every bone in her frail body was aching to come with us but she knew she had to stay. This was her only option.

'She looks terrified,' I said to Claire as we walked back to our cars.

'She'll soon settle in,' she replied. 'She's safe and that's the main thing. Now she can start to rebuild a life away from Martin.'

Claire had arranged to come back to my house after the refuge so we could talk about Hailey's parenting assessment and how it was going to go.

'Neil, the IRO, and I both feel that a seven-week assessment will be enough this time, given that she's already done a few weeks previously,' she said.

Claire also explained how she felt the assessment would be best split between my house and the refuge.

'You and I both know that refuges can be quite intense places. There are lots of women there dealing with trauma and it can be quite hard going at times. I think it would be a relief for Hailey to do some of the assessment at your house.'

'I agree,' I said. 'I think she'd relish the peace and quiet so she can just spend time with Jasmine.'

We decided that I'd drop Jasmine off at the refuge three mornings a week and Jan the contact worker and Hailey would spend a couple of hours with her. Then two mornings a week they'd do the same at my house.

Before the assessment officially started, I took Jasmine into the refuge every day to see Hailey and I could see she was struggling. She had been at the refuge for five days when Liz, her keyworker, pulled me to one side.

'I'm worried about Hailey,' she told me. 'She's very quiet and she spends a lot of time alone in her room. She doesn't talk to anyone or mix with the other women.'

'I'll have a chat to her,' I told her.

I knew exactly what the problem was. Rather than relishing her freedom, Hailey didn't know what to do with herself. Martin had controlled her and her life for so long, she didn't know how to be around other people. She'd been cut off from her friends and family and she was hardly allowed to leave the house. Being in a busy refuge with lots of other women must be so overwhelming and difficult for her. I knew it took Hailey a long time to feel confident and secure enough to speak to strangers. It had taken her months to start opening up to me.

'How are you finding it here?' I asked her, when we sat down with a cup of tea later that morning on our own.

'It's so noisy and busy and people are always asking me questions,' she replied, hugging her mug of tea to herself. 'They talk all the time to each other about what happened to them but I can't bring myself to join in.'

'Why?' I asked.

'Because it's still too raw and also I'm ashamed,' she said. 'I'm ashamed that I let Martin hurt me like that. Ashamed that my baby's been taken away from me.'

'You've got absolutely nothing to be ashamed of, Hailey,' I told her. 'You don't have to talk to anyone if you don't feel ready. But it would be nice for you to have a bit of company – even if it's just going downstairs, making yourself a cup of coffee and drinking it in the kitchen rather than taking it back up to your room.'

'Some of the girls sit and watch *EastEnders* together on a night,' she volunteered.

'There you go,' I smiled. 'It might be nice for you to join them one evening.'

'OK, I promise I'll try,' she shrugged.

I could see Hailey was finding being on her own a struggle and she seemed quite dispirited.

'Maggie, when will I be able to live with my baby again?' she asked me suddenly. 'I've done everything everyone asked me to. I've left Martin and I'm on my own now. I chose Jasmine over him just like you all wanted me to. I don't understand why you're making me jump through more hoops and do another assessment.'

She sounded very fed up.

'Hailey, Social Services has got to be absolutely sure that you're not going to go back to Martin,' I told her. 'Imagine if Jasmine came to live with you then she had to go back into care because you'd changed your mind? That would be so unsettling for her after everything she's been through.'

'But honestly, I'm not going to go back,' she sighed. 'Why won't anyone believe me?'

'It's not about us believing you,' I replied. 'It's about Social Services being able to show the courts with absolute conviction that you've left your violent partner for good and that you're capable of looking after not only your baby but yourself.'

Hailey put her head in her hands and shook her head.

'Sometimes I think . . . '

Then she stopped herself.

'No, go on,' I said. 'Sometimes you think what?'

She looked down at the floor.

'Sometimes I think it would be easier to just stop all this and go back to Martin.'

'What?!' I gasped, truly horrified. 'You don't mean that, do you? After all you've been through?'

'I miss him, Maggie,' she replied, looking very unsure of herself. 'And I'm not sure how much more of this I can take . . . '

SIXTEEN

A Wobble

I couldn't believe what I was hearing. After everything that she'd been through Hailey was considering going back to the man who had beaten her to a pulp, left her for dead and put her in hospital for over a week.

The reality was, I knew there was nothing I could do to stop her if that's what she really wanted. The refuge wasn't a prison. Hailey could come and go as she pleased, so there was nothing stopping her getting up one day, walking out and going back to Martin and her old life.

Hailey must have noticed the horrified look on my face.

'I know you think I'm mad, Maggie, but sometimes I think going back to him would be the easier option,' she continued. 'I don't feel free, I just feel frightened.'

'I do understand, Hailey,' I told her, trying to remain calm despite the turmoil I felt inside. 'It might feel easier to you to go back to him, but you need to think about what you will lose if you do. You will lose Jasmine – there's no doubt about that.

'I know everything must feel so scary for you right now but it will pass. You've done the hard bit. You've left him.'

I reflected sadly that I should not be surprised by Hailey's change of heart. I had seen this happen many times before with women who had suffered domestic violence. They left their abusive partner and everything seemed so overwhelming that eventually they went back. How does the old saying go? Better the devil you know than the devil you don't.

I phoned Claire when I got home from the refuge.

'I think Hailey's having a wobble,' I told her. 'She's very low and she was talking today about going back to Martin.'

'What?' she sighed. 'After everything he's done to her. After everything she said about fighting for Jasmine?'

'You and I know it's never that simple,' I told her.

'Well, I'm afraid what happened today isn't going to help matters,' Claire said.

Claire explained that Martin had turned up at Social Services that afternoon and left a letter for Hailey at reception and a note to Claire asking her to pass it on.

'Will you give it to her?' I asked.

'Yes, of course,' she said. 'I have to.

'I can imagine that it's full of grovelling and him begging her to take him back, which is not going to help if she's wavering.'

'All we can do is be brutally honest with her about what she has to lose,' I said. 'And then the choice is in her hands.'

Claire wanted us both to be at the refuge when she gave the letter to Hailey.

'She might not want to open it in front of us,' I told her.

'I think it would be good for us to be there for moral support in case she needs it,' Claire replied.

Claire arranged to come up to the refuge in the morning when I was there dropping off Jasmine.

'I wanted to pop in today to give you this,' she told Hailey. She handed her a small white envelope.

Hailey stared at it. 'What is it?' she asked suspiciously.

'It's a letter from Martin,' Claire replied. 'He came into Social Services yesterday and asked if we could pass it on to you.'

Hailey didn't say a word. She took the envelope and sat staring at it in her lap.

'Are you all right?' Claire asked. 'I can keep it for you until you're ready to read it, if you want?'

'No,' she muttered. 'If Martin wanted me to have it then I'll open it.'

I noticed her hands were shaking as she ripped it open. It was a single side of paper and as she read it, tears streamed down her face.

Claire and I gave each other a worried look.

'I'll go and make us all a cup of tea,' she said.

When Claire had gone downstairs to the kitchen, I went and sat next to Hailey on her bed.

'Are you OK?' I asked her. 'What has he said to you?'

I could imagine exactly what would be in it – he'd declare his undying love, tell her he'd changed and beg her to come home.

She handed me the letter and I quickly glanced through it.

I'm trying so hard to change and I'm truly sorry. I didn't mean to hurt you, I was just so frustrated about Jasmine being taken off us and all the hoops we were having to jump

through. This has all happened because of Social Services.
You, me and Jasmine were happy before they started
meddling into our business and I'm so upset about what
they've done to us. I love and miss you so much Hailey.

I could feel my hackles rising as I read it. He was preying on all her weaknesses.

'These are the nicest things he's ever said to me,' she sighed, her eyes shiny with tears. 'You see, Maggie, he does love me.'

All I could do was be blunt.

'Hailey, he's only saying this because he's trying to get you to come back so you don't press charges against him,' I told her.

'How do you know?' she snapped. 'You've had it in for him from the beginning.'

'Because sadly I've come across too many men like Martin and I know what they're like,' I said, trying to sound calm and measured.

'Hailey, your bruises have barely healed and you're considering going back to a man who hurt you that badly. You could have died that night. If you go back to him he will hurt you again and make you suffer even more.'

'It's my choice,' she sobbed. 'I'm scared about being on my own and I'm lonely.'

'You're right, it is your choice,' I said. 'And your choice is very simple. The reality is, if you go back to Martin you will never get your daughter back. You will lose Jasmine once and for all, Hailey. No second chances.'

I could see she thought I was being cruel but I was incredibly frustrated. We were back to square one again, at exactly the same point we'd been at a couple of weeks ago before Martin had attacked Hailey.

'You know, Maggie, there are some women here who stay at the refuge for a bit and then they go back home to their partners,' Hailey told me. 'They say they've changed. People do change, you know.'

'I wonder how many of those women end up coming back into a refuge when they get hurt again,' I said. 'And how many of those women have got their children living with them.'

Hailey looked at Jasmine, who was sitting playing with some toys on the bedroom floor.

'They still see their kids but they don't live with them any more,' she muttered.

'Hailey, is that honestly what you want? I thought you wanted to make a life with Jasmine. To be there on her first day at school, see her take her first steps and push her on a swing in the park?'

'I do,' she sobbed. 'I do. It's just so hard.'

I held her as she sobbed in my arms. Although I was frustrated that she was taking a backwards step, I really felt for her. I could see she was being pulled in every direction.

Claire came back in with a tray of tea.

'I'm not going to keep harping on at you about it, Hailey,' I said. I put my hands on her shoulders and looked at her squarely in the eye. 'I can't keep going over and over the same things.

'You know what's at risk here and there's nothing else Claire or I can say.

'Nobody is stopping you from going back to your husband but it means that you will lose your daughter.'

It was hard and incredibly frustrating sometimes as a foster carer to have to sit back and let people make their own decisions – especially if it was, in my eyes, the wrong one. Hailey was so vulnerable and she felt like she had no one in her life but Martin. I wanted to shake her and beg not to do it, not to be so stupid as to fall for his lies. But I couldn't. All I could do was point out what was at stake.

'Maggie's right,' Claire told her. 'If you go back to Martin then that will be it. Social Services will have no choice but to immediately cancel your assessment and Jasmine will start the adoption process.'

They were the cold facts.

As promised, over the next few days none of us talked about it again but it was always there, niggling at the back of my mind. When I took Jasmine to the refuge in the mornings, half of me wondered whether Hailey would actually still be there. Mercifully, so far she always was.

I knew she was still finding it hard, but I thought the refuge was a good safety net for her. Hailey needed the support the refuge provided, and she needed to build up her self-confidence as well as having help with practical things. She'd lived in isolation for so long she didn't know how to do a supermarket shop or pay a gas bill.

She spent her first week there sorting out practical things before her assessment officially started. She'd left home with nothing and had no documents, so Liz helped her find out her National Insurance number, set up a bank account and register for income support so she had some money of her own.

One morning I turned up to find her bouncing around with excitement.

'Look, Maggie, I've got a bank card!' she said. 'I've never had one of those before.'

One of the other women had given her their old purse to keep her card and money in, and Hailey was over the moon. It made me realise how incredibly naive she was. She'd been through so much that it was sometimes easy to forget she was only in her early twenties.

In between my trips back and forth to the refuge, the twins' adoption was also moving forward. One day, while the girls were at school, Helen bought Lizzie and Joe round to meet me. They weren't allowed to be introduced to Daisy and Polly until they'd been approved at panel and we were sure everything was going to go ahead, but I thought it would be nice for them to find out more about the girls and see where they were living.

When they walked in I was struck by what a good-looking couple they were. They were like something out of a magazine advert. Joe was a handsome businessman in a suit and tie and Lizzie was beautifully made up with glossy red fingernails and very white teeth. Daisy and Polly were like two little magpies and they loved sparkly jewellery, handbags and make-up. I knew they'd love Lizzie.

I could tell she and Joe were very nervous but keen to make a good impression.

'I'll give you a quick tour of the house,' I told them. 'I thought you might like to see the girls' room and some of their favourite toys.'

It would help them build up a picture of the twins in their heads before they were able to meet them in person.

'I have to warn you they're very girly girls so there's pink everywhere, I'm afraid,' I told them.

'Don't worry, I'm partial to a bit of pink myself,' smiled Joe.

As they relaxed and opened up a bit more over a cup of coffee, I could see they were nice, genuine people. They both had a sadness around the fact they didn't have children in their lives, and they were already very emotionally invested in the twins. It was always a relief to me when I liked my children's adopters and got on with them. That wasn't always the case.

I also wanted to make them aware that things might be testing for a while after they brought the girls home.

'Hopefully you've read the reports and Helen has talked to you about how the girls were when they first came to live with me.'

Joe looked at Helen and nodded.

'I was in tears reading what they went through,' sighed Lizzie. 'Poor little loves. How could anyone treat their own children like that?'

She was right, it was heartbreaking, and seeing children who had been seriously neglected was not something that I would ever get used to.

'The girls have been doing brilliantly,' I told them. 'They've settled into school better than I'd ever imagined, and they seem so excited about getting a new mummy and daddy.'

Joe and Lizzie smiled at each other.

'But it's also important to remember that this will be another massive change for them and it will probably bring up lots of their old feelings about their birth parents.

'It will be scary for them and they'll be unsettled, so they might regress and revert back to some of their old behaviours.

Toilet training might go to pot, they might have tantrums or issues with food. It's hard to tell how it will affect them.'

Joe and Lizzie didn't seem deterred.

'We've talked about that with Helen and we know it's going to be hard going at first, but we're prepared for that,' said Lizzie. 'We really want the girls and we want them to be happy.'

'I'll always be here to help if you need me, too,' I said.

I had a really warm feeling about Joe and Lizzie and I knew they could give the girls a good home.

'It was lovely to meet you,' I told them as I saw them out to the door. 'And the next time I see you it will hopefully be to start planning how we're going to settle the girls in with you.'

'Yes,' said Helen. 'We're hoping they'll go to panel in the next week or so, so they have a decision before Christmas.'

Christmas. Only a couple of weeks away, it was also at the forefront of my mind. I was particularly concerned about where Hailey was going to go. I knew there would be a big Christmas dinner at the refuge, but I knew how difficult she found social situations and I thought she might feel more relaxed and comfortable spending it at my house.

I knew I needed to talk it over with Claire before I even mentioned it to Hailey.

'I wanted to ask you if I could invite Hailey over to my house on Christmas Day to spend time with Jasmine.'

'If she wants to, then I don't see why not,' she said, smiling at the thought.

A week before Christmas, I took Hailey a little pressie up to the refuge.

'I brought you something,' I told her, smiling.

I gave her a carrier bag and inside was a small potted Christmas tree and a clear Perspex bauble that I'd put a photo of Jasmine into.

'I thought it would help brighten up your room and make you feel festive.'

'Thank you,' she replied. She seemed genuinely touched, yet there was something gloomy about her. 'I really appreciate it, but to be honest I don't feel very Christmassy at all.'

She put the Christmas tree on her windowsill and twiddled with the bauble.

'Actually I wanted to talk to you about that,' I said. 'How would you feel about coming to my house on Christmas Day and spending it with Jasmine?'

'What, the whole day?' she gasped, her eyes wide with hope. 'Would that be allowed?'

'I've already run it past Claire and she's agreed that you can do that if you want. But I won't be offended if you'd rather spend it here at the refuge.'

'No, no way,' she quickly replied. 'I can't believe it. I'd love to come to your house.'

She laughed and it warmed my heart to see she was genuinely delighted.

'I also asked Claire if you could have your contact session with Jasmine at my house on Christmas Eve instead of here. I've agreed with her that I can drop you back in the evening so you can stay a bit later and help put Jasmine to bed. That way I can also rope you into helping me and Louisa do the kids' stockings.'

'That would be brilliant,' Hailey replied, looking the happiest I'd ever seen her.

'You won't be saying that when I give you a mountain of presents to wrap,' I laughed.

Claire had agreed that a taxi could bring Hailey over to my house on Christmas Day and I'd drop her back at the refuge in the evening while Louisa babysat.

I wanted Hailey to feel part of Jasmine's first Christmas and now it seemed she genuinely couldn't wait.

The days flew by and soon it was Christmas Eve. I actually prefer the 24th to Christmas Day itself. I love all the preparation and the sense of anticipation.

When the taxi dropped Hailey off, our house was a bustle of activity. The radio was blasting out Christmas songs, I had some mince pies in the oven and the girls were as high as kites with excitement. The Christmas lights were twinkling on the huge tree in the living room and on every surface there was some sort of singing Santa or dancing reindeer.

'Wow,' gasped Hailey. 'It looks so festive in here.'

'I love Christmas,' I smiled. 'I'm like a big kid.'

Hailey was happy to spend the day being with Jasmine and playing with her. Just after lunch my mobile rang. It was Polly and Daisy's adoption worker, Helen.

'Sorry to bother you on Christmas Eve, but I wanted to pass on some good news,' she said. 'Lizzie and Joe went to panel yesterday and they've been approved to adopt the twins.'

'That's brilliant,' I said. 'How did they take it?'

'Oh, they are absolutely over the moon,' she chuckled. 'I think it's made their Christmas.

'Have a lovely Christmas, Maggie, and I'll be in touch after the holiday to start planning the next steps.'

'Merry Christmas, Helen,' I said, my heart full of festive cheer.

I really liked Joe and Lizzie and I was so happy for the twins. I desperately wished I could share the news with the girls as I was so excited, but I knew I had to keep it to myself. Little did they know, the best Christmas present they could hope for was waiting.

The rest of the afternoon passed by in a blur. I let Hailey take the lead in looking after Jasmine. She fed her tea and then gave her a bath and put her in the reindeer Babygro that I'd bought for her.

'Before she goes to bed let me get a photo of the two of you in front of the Christmas tree,' I told her.

Hailey cuddled her daughter and smiled while I clicked away on my camera phone.

'That's one for Jasmine's memory book,' I said.

It was important for both of them that they had a reminder of Jasmine's first Christmas. It was also important for Hailey to have some nice memories, too. She hadn't had many of those in the past few years.

'Could I get a copy of it?' asked Hailey. 'I don't have many photos of Jasmine. Martin wouldn't let me take any.'

'Of course you can,' I said. 'Wherever Jasmine goes to live, her memory book will go with her.'

I made a Christmas wish that Jasmine's home would be with Hailey.

Hailey put Jasmine to bed and then she joined me and Louisa at the kitchen table. There was a mountain of presents, countless rolls of wrapping paper and two rolls of Sellotape.

'There's so much stuff to wrap, we're going to be here until midnight,' wailed Louisa. 'Thank God you're here to help, Hailey!'

I made us all a cup of tea and a plate of mince pies and we got stuck in.

'These are for Jasmine's stocking,' I said, showing Hailey some wooden toys and picture books. I'd also got her an activity table that played music and made noises when you pushed the buttons.

'Oh, she's going to love that,' said Hailey. 'I bought her a couple of little things, too. They're not much but my first lot of income support came through.'

She'd got her a rag doll and a wooden shape sorter.

'They're absolutely lovely,' I replied, giving her a reassuring smile.

As we wrapped, we chatted and drank our tea.

'Liz says I can go on the housing list and maybe in a few months I can get a council property,' Hailey told me. 'So hopefully this time next year I'll be wrapping Jasmine's presents in my own place.'

I grinned at her.

'Why are you smiling at me like that?' she asked.

'Because what you've just told me means that you've made your decision, haven't you?'

Hailey nodded.

'Yes,' she said. 'I'm not going back to him, Maggie. I want my daughter back too much. I've chosen her and I always will. I don't want Martin to hurt us any more.'

I reached over and squeezed her hand. I didn't want to make a big scene but inside I was absolutely ecstatic.

'I threw Martin's letter away in the end,' said Hailey nervously. 'Has Claire heard any more from him?'

'Not that I know of,' I replied. 'But I know she's waiting to hear from the police if he's pleading guilty to assault, or whether there's going to be a trial or not.'

'I hope not,' said Hailey, a dark shadow passing over her face. 'The thought of that makes me feel sick.'

'Well, let's not worry about that now,' I said. 'You've made your decision so you concentrate on enjoying your first Christmas with your baby.'

As we got on with our wrapping, I was struck by an overwhelming sense of relief. For the first time in a long while I truly felt as if things were finally working out.

SEVENTEEN

Christmas and Courts

It was Christmas Day, we'd all been up since 6 a.m., and the house was already in chaos. There was wrapping paper strewn all over the floor and cardboard boxes everywhere. Poppy and Daisy were still in their pyjamas as they excitedly played with their new toys.

'I'm just going to put Jasmine down for a nap,' I told Louisa over the racket. 'That means she'll be awake when Hailey arrives.'

We'd saved all of her presents so Hailey could open them with her when she got here. Her taxi dropped her off just after 10 a.m.

'Merry Christmas,' I smiled. 'Come in and have a cup of tea. Jasmine will be awake soon.'

As if on cue, ten minutes later we heard crying from upstairs.

'You can go up and get her if you want,' I said. 'There's a clean nappy on the side and I've laid a little Christmas dress out that you can put her in.'

I'd left Jasmine in the reindeer Babygro that Hailey had dressed her in the night before. That way when she went to get her up it would feel special that she was getting her dressed for Christmas morning.

Ten minutes later Hailey proudly carried Jasmine downstairs.

'Oh, look at your beautiful little girl,' I said.

'She does look really cute in this dress,' agreed Hailey, her face lit up by a wide grin.

The twins were as excited about Jasmine's presents as they had been about their own. We all gathered round as Hailey opened the gifts for Jasmine from her stocking.

'I've got a little something for you, too,' I said, handing Hailey a box.

I'm very practical when it comes to buying presents for people and I'd got her a kettle for her room and a couple of nice mugs.

'You can take them with you when you leave the refuge and get your own place,' I told her.

'Thank you, Maggie, that's really thoughtful,' she said, and I thought I detected the slight shimmer of a tear in her eye.

I'd also got her some toiletries and a make-up bag and Louisa had bought her some mascara and blusher.

'I love them! But I've got no idea what to do with make-up,' laughed Hailey.

'I can show you later if you want,' replied Louisa.

It was a day of happiness and laughter and I think Hailey was the most relaxed I'd ever seen her as she sat next to Jasmine in her high chair at the table. We pulled endless crackers and after turkey and all the trimmings we were stuffed.

Later in the afternoon Louisa gave Hailey a make-up lesson and the twins couldn't resist joining in. They kept coming in to show me their pink lipstick or the bright circles of blusher they'd dabbed onto their cheeks.

'Oh, lovely,' I chuckled. 'Very pretty.'

Then we all settled down to watch a film. Louisa popped her head around the living-room door.

'I'm going to go round to Charlie's now,' she said. 'But I'll be back by 9 p.m. That's not too late, is it?'

'Is that all right with you, Hailey?' I asked. 'Is it OK if I drop you back after 9 p.m.?'

'Yeah, brilliant,' she replied. 'That means I can put Jasmine to bed again.'

This was the first time in months that she'd seen her daughter for longer than a few hours and she was relishing every minute of it.

When the girls had gone to bed Hailey helped me tidy up. We filled a couple of bin bags with bits of crackers, cardboard and wrapping paper. I made us a cup of tea and we flopped down on the settee.

'Wow, I'm exhausted,' I sighed. 'But it's been a good day.'

I looked over at Hailey.

'Have you had a nice day, lovey?' I asked her. 'Are you glad you came?'

Tears suddenly streamed down her face.

'Don't worry, I'm fine,' she smiled, wiping her face self-consciously with her sleeve. 'It's been lovely. I'm just so happy and grateful. I can't remember having a Christmas like this since I was tiny.'

'I'm glad you've enjoyed it,' I told her, my heart swelling with sympathy for this poor woman who'd had so little joy in her life. 'I hope you and Jasmine have many, many more together.'

'So do I,' she replied, sinking back into the sofa.

When Louisa came back from Charlie's I drove Hailey to the refuge. I could tell she wasn't looking forward to going back. She was very quiet in the car.

I pulled up outside and she hesitated before she got out.

'Thank you for everything, Maggie,' she said, turning to face me, her eyes wet with a fresh batch of tears.

I gave her hand a reassuring squeeze before she climbed out. I waited in the car as she pressed the intercom. When the door opened, she turned around and waved before going in. I knew it would feel strange for her going back to her room on her own after spending the day with us and her baby. But I was so pleased she had been able to come and spend some special time with Jasmine. I could see it had given her a desperately needed boost and showed her that she and Jasmine could make their own memories safely away from Martin.

I drove home and for the first time all day I finally had a moment to myself, so I gave Graham a call. We'd swapped texts first thing that morning, but I wanted to speak to him in person.

'Merry Christmas,' I told him when he answered his mobile. 'How's your day been?'

'I had a great time at my sister's,' he said. 'I've eaten too much though. And what about you?'

'You know what? It's been a really lovely day,' I sighed, happily. 'Better than I ever expected. The girls had a ball and we had a really nice lunch.'

We chit-chatted about presents and what we'd watched on telly.

'I've still got your pressie here, Maggie,' he told me, and I felt a pang of guilt for neglecting him over the last few months.

'I know, I know,' I sighed. 'And I've got a little something for you. I'm so sorry that I've hardly seen you. Things have been so hectic here. The twins are about to go for adoption in the new year and I'm helping a mum who's going through a really hard time.'

'I understand,' he told me. 'You warned me from the start that your job is 24/7, so you don't need to feel bad. It would be great to meet up in the new year, though.'

'We will,' I replied. 'I promise.'

Before I went to bed I sorted out some photographs of the twins to send to Joe and Lizzie. They'd given me their email address when they came round so that I could send them regular updates about how the twins were and what they'd been up to. I emailed them some pictures of the girls opening their presents and told them what they'd got in their stockings. Even though they hadn't met them in person yet, I wanted them to feel like they were already part of their lives.

Christmas had been a break from reality for all of us but as the new year dawned I could see Hailey's old anxieties creeping back. She was still waiting to hear whether or not Martin had pleaded guilty to assaulting her, and the thought of a possible trial was niggling at her.

Claire offered to call the police and chase it up for her.

'I've already phoned them,' said Hailey. 'They said every-thing had been delayed because of Christmas but that he was due to enter a plea this month. They promised they'd ring me if there was any news.'

I prayed that Martin would do the right thing and admit what he'd done. The last thing Hailey needed was the stress of a trial hanging over her.

Now it was the new year, her new parental assessment was officially starting. Each week Jan would see her at the refuge three mornings and at my house twice. I'd drop Jasmine off at the refuge and leave Jan and Hailey to it. I only had a sense of how it was going when they were at my house.

'How's she getting on?' I asked Jan one morning a couple of weeks into the new routine, when Hailey was changing Jasmine upstairs.

'Honestly, Maggie, she's doing brilliantly,' she said. 'She loves her baby and she knows how to look after her. She's a lot more relaxed and confident when she's at your house though. Things are a little bit more strained when we're at the refuge.'

'That's understandable,' I said. 'There are always people around and lots of dramas and comings and goings. I know Hailey still finds it hard to socialise with the other women.'

She was familiar with my house, she felt safe here and she knew where everything was.

I could see for myself that Hailey was a good mum and Jasmine was flourishing. She was eight months old now and she had turned into such a happy, chatty, wriggly little thing. She was still petite and low down the percentile chart weight-wise, but she had started to take more food and the health visitor wasn't worried. She was catching up with her milestones like sitting up, babbling and playing with toys.

She knew who her mummy was, too. She'd flap her arms in excitement when Hailey arrived and she'd go to her easily. Her anxiety had gone now Martin wasn't around. She was picking up on the fact that her mummy was relaxed, so she was relaxed too.

One morning Hailey came round and Jasmine held her arms out to her.

'You two have a little play and I'll make us a coffee before Jan arrives,' I told her.

I was in the kitchen when I heard Hailey shouting.

'Maggie, Maggie, come quick!'

The spoon dropped into the sink with a clatter as I dashed into the living room. There, in the middle of the room with a big smile on her face, was Jasmine on all fours.

'She just crawled!' beamed Hailey. 'She just did it then right in front of me.'

'That's brilliant,' I said, laughing off the panic I'd felt only a moment previously. 'She's been trying to for the past few days but she was obviously saving it to show her mummy.'

I was so pleased for Hailey that she had been there when Jasmine reached a milestone.

Later that morning we were all surprised when Claire popped in.

'I wanted to come round and see how things were going,' she said. Then she hesitated.

'And I also wanted to give you this, Hailey.'

I felt sick with dread as I saw the white envelope.

'Is it from him?' Hailey asked, her face suddenly pale. 'Is it from Martin?'

Claire gave a grim nod.

'I believe so.'

Hailey took it from her and then, much to my surprise, ripped it up into pieces.

'Can you put this in the bin for me, Maggie?' she asked. 'I'm not even going to read it. There's no point. I've got no time for his lies anymore.'

Then she turned on her heels and went back to playing with Jasmine. Claire and I exchanged a look of relief. She couldn't have been more different to the Hailey who nearly threw it all in only a couple of weeks ago.

The new year meant it was also time to start the settling-in process with the twins and their new parents. With Pat, their social worker, and Helen, the adoption worker, Joe, Lizzie and I all sat down and decided how it was going to be done.

'We'll do it over nine days,' Helen began. 'I'll come and see the girls tomorrow and tell them all about you and then you can meet them next week.'

'Why don't you pop in for a cup of tea after school one afternoon?' I suggested.

'Sounds good,' said Joe.

'I can't wait,' added Lizzie. They exchanged broad smiles.

Helen came round the following day to speak to Polly and Daisy.

'Remember when I talked to you about how we were looking for a new mummy and daddy for you both?'

The girls nodded, their little faces turned up at her expectantly.

'Well, the good news is we've found you one. I've been to see your new mummy and daddy and I've told them all about you. And they really, really want to meet you.

'Do you want to see a picture of them? They've sent a photo album so you can see them and their house. Shall we have a look at it?'

'Yeah!' said Daisy, jumping up and down with excitement.

Polly looked hesitant, but she soon cheered up when she saw a picture of Lizzie.

'She's very pretty,' she sighed. 'And I like her red fingernails.'

'I love nail varnish,' squealed Daisy. 'Our new mummy wears nail varnish.'

They were even more excited when they saw a photo of the garden with a swing in it, and one of a cat.

'I love kitty cats,' said Polly.

'Your new mummy and daddy told me his name is Mr Tiddles,' Helen told them and they both laughed.

'That's a funny name,' said Daisy.

Helen answered their torrent of questions patiently, and each answer she gave seemed to meet the twins' approval. With a light heart, I showed Helen out.

'That went well,' Helen said.

'Yes they seem really excited,' I replied. 'If you're speaking to Lizzie later today will you ask her to bring some kids' nail varnish with her when she comes to meet them?'

'Oh yes, good idea, Maggie. The girls will love that!'

On the morning they were due to come round, I broke the news to the girls.

'Guess what? Your new mummy and daddy are going to pop round for a cup of tea after school today. Would you like that?'

The girls nodded, grinning at one another. When Lizzie and Joe arrived that night I could see they were both buzzing with nervous excitement.

'The twins are looking forward to meeting you,' I told them.

I took them into the kitchen where the girls were being creative with some Hama beads.

'Look who's here to see you,' I said. 'This is Joe and Lizzie, your new mummy and daddy.'

'Hi, Polly and Daisy!' said Lizzie. 'What are you up to?'

Both the twins were quite shy at first and wouldn't even make eye contact with them. I was prepared for this.

'Girls, why don't Lizzie and Joe sit down with you and you can show them how to do the beads?' I suggested.

As Lizzie pulled up a chair and sat down, Polly noticed her nails.

'Look at your nails,' she gasped. 'They're really shiny. Can I touch them?'

'Of course you can,' Lizzie told her. 'I've actually got some nail varnish in my bag. I could paint your fingernails too if you want?'

'Ooh, yes please,' said Daisy. 'Will you do mine?'

They both sat there transfixed as Lizzie painted their nails with glittery pink children's polish. When Daisy had had hers done she walked over to Joe and shyly showed him her fingers.

'Oh, they look lovely,' he said, beaming with pride.

He'd hung back a little bit and hadn't said much up until now. It was often harder for the man as little girls were sometimes more wary of them. Jasmine was crawling around the floor with some toys, and Joe had started building a tower with some Duplo.

'Be careful of the baby,' Polly warned him. 'She'll probably knock it over. She does that. Do you want me to help you?'

'Oh, yes please,' he said. 'You can help me make it really strong and stable so the baby can't destroy it.'

Joe and Lizzie had bought the girls a little teddy each for their bedrooms.

'I know, why don't you each choose a cuddly toy to give to your new mummy and daddy,' I suggested. 'Then they can take it back to your new house and put it in your new bedrooms and you can go and see them next week.'

As far as first meetings go, I thought it had gone really well. I could tell that Joe and Lizzie were smitten with the girls. They couldn't stop looking at them and smiling.

'Oh, Maggie, they're such gorgeous girls,' whispered Lizzie on the way out. 'I feel so lucky to be given the opportunity to be their mummy.'

I could see she was close to tears.

'And thank you for the nail varnish idea,' she said. 'That went down so well.'

'No problem, Lizzie. We'll see you tomorrow,' I told them, smiling.

The rest of the week couldn't have gone any better. The following day Lizzie and Joe came round and stayed for tea, then the day after that they came with me to pick them up from school. Normally I'd take a child out of school when we were settling them with new parents, but because the twins were staying at the same school, it was important to include it in the process.

A couple of days after that, Joe and Lizzie came early in the morning to get the girls ready for school and then dropped them off themselves. I rang the girls' teacher, Mrs Nevil, to check that there hadn't been any issues.

'They seem fine,' she said. 'Really happy and confident. They've told the rest of the class about their new mummy and daddy, and they were really excited that they were picking them up the other day.'

'That's great to hear,' I replied, smiling with relief.

It all seemed to be working out perfectly. I was glad, but in fact a part of me was also worried about how easily they had coped. I discussed my fears with Becky.

'I'm worried they're being carried along with the excitement of having a new mummy and daddy and the real problems will start once the novelty wears off.'

'They could do,' Becky replied. 'But remember, children their age are very accepting and cope with change quite well.'

It was true. A lot of people thought adoptions worked well with four- and five-year-olds because they were old enough to understand what was happening to them yet they were still very adaptable.

'It doesn't mean to say there are not going to be problems in the future, but as long as the adoptive parents are aware of it, that's all you can do.'

I knew she was right. I couldn't help but worry as I wanted the best for the girls.

That weekend, the twins were due to go to Lizzie and Joe's house for the first time so I sorted more of their things for them to take. When Hailey came round she saw all the boxes piled up in the hallway.

'What are all the boxes for?' she asked.

'The twins are going to live with their adoptive parents soon. I'm sorting some of their stuff out so they can start taking it over.'

'Aw, that's lovely,' she said. 'I'm really pleased for them.'

'I am too,' I said. 'They seem really happy.'

Hailey suddenly looked really reticent.

'What is it, lovey?' I asked.

'Oh, I was just thinking that it could just as easily have been Jasmine that you were packing for. If I had gone back to Martin then she could have been moving to adoptive parents.'

'That's true,' I said. 'But thankfully things have worked out differently for Jasmine. Her mummy is fighting to keep her.'

Hailey gave me a weak smile.

'Do you think I'll ever get her back, Maggie?' she sighed. 'Do you think she can come home with me soon? This assessment feels like it's going on forever.'

'Well, you have feedback meetings with Claire and Jan every week. What are they saying to you?'

'They say everything's going really well,'

'Then the signs are good,' I told her. 'You've just got to be patient.'

I knew Claire was also keen for Hailey to get the sentencing out of the way before anything definite was decided about Jasmine's future.

A couple of hours later, Hailey was getting ready to go back to the refuge and Jan and I were chatting in the kitchen when Hailey's mobile rang.

Both Jan and I saw her face drain of colour when she heard who was on the other end.

'Yes, it is Hailey,' she said.

She listened.

'Oh, OK,' she told the caller. 'Thanks. Thank you for letting me know.'

She hung up and looked like she was going to pass out.

'Hailey, are you OK?' I asked, rushing to her side. 'Who was that?'

She looked stunned and didn't say anything.

'Oh my God, you're shaking,' said Jan. 'Come and sit down.'

We steered her towards the sofa. She collapsed onto it, put her head in her hands and burst into tears. Jan and I looked at each other in alarm.

'Hailey, you've got to tell us what's just happened. Who was that you were talking to?'

'It was the police,' she said. 'They were updating me about Martin.'

My heart sank. It must have been bad news.

'He's pleaded guilty to assaulting me, Maggie,' she said, her face the picture of disbelief. 'That means there's not going to be a trial and I don't have to give evidence. He's admitted that he hurt me.'

'What?' I gasped. 'Well, that's brilliant news, isn't it? That's what you were hoping for.'

'I know,' she said. 'I can hardly believe it. I'd convinced myself that he was going to deny it and I'd have to go to court. That means it's going to be over soon, Maggie, and I can finally move on with my life.'

EIGHTEEN

Goodbyes

Each day that passed was one day closer to the twins leaving for good. I had that strange mix of feelings I always did when a child left my house. The twins had been through so much and they'd lived with me for almost a year. I was happy for them that they'd found their forever family, but at the same time I felt an overwhelming sense of loss. I knew Louisa felt it too.

'It's weird, isn't it, thinking that they won't be here by the end of the week,' she sighed as I made dinner. 'I'm going to miss their little faces so much.'

'I know,' I sighed. 'The house is going to seem very quiet with only Jasmine in it.'

And I knew Jasmine was going to miss them too. She absolutely adored the twins and her eyes would follow them around the room, watching what they were doing. It was going to be a big upheaval for us all.

The girls' first visit to their new home went really well and they came back so excited.

'Our bedroom was the pinkest in the whole world,' said Daisy.

'Yeah, and our house has got a cat,' added Polly. 'He's called Mr Tiddles and he let me stroke him.'

'Oh yes,' I smiled. 'I remember seeing a photo of him in the album that your new mummy and daddy sent.'

I was pleased to hear both girls now referred to it as 'our house'.

I'd sorted their stuff into boxes and had started gradually sending it over with Joe and Lizzie.

'Which box is for the baby?' asked Polly one night. 'Where are her things?'

'Which baby, lovey?' I asked, confused.

'Jasmine, silly! She'll need her things too when she comes to live with our new mummy and daddy.'

'Oh, sweetheart, Jasmine isn't going with you,' I said. 'She's staying here.'

Polly looked like she was about to burst into tears.

'But why?' asked Daisy. 'Why can't the baby come? We can share our new mummy and daddy with her.'

'She's got her own mummy, remember?' I said. 'You've met Jasmine's mummy – Hailey.'

I could see they were getting things straight in their heads.

That weekend they were spending the night for the first time at their new house, and then on the Monday Lizzie and Joe were picking them up from school and bringing them here to say a final goodbye. The nine-day settling in had gone very quickly and smoothly.

The night before they left for good we had their favourite tea – fish and chips from the local chip shop. Then afterwards we all played a game of Hungry Hippos.

'Remember what's happening tomorrow?' I asked them as I tucked them into bed that night. 'Your new mummy and daddy are going to pick you up from school and then they'll bring you back here so you can say bye to me, Jasmine and Louisa.

'And then you're going to sleep at your new house forever and ever. Isn't that brilliant?'

Both girls nodded but I could see it was all becoming very real for them.

'But Maggie, I'll miss you,' said Polly in a quiet voice, her little eyes wide.

'Of course you'll miss me and I'll miss you both enormously,' I told her, brushing her cheek.

'I will still be here and you'll only be down the road in your new house and we'll still see each other. In a few weeks, can I come round and meet Mr Tiddles and see your new bedroom?'

Both girls nodded and gave me a smile. It took all my strength to not show them the tears that were threatening to fall.

The following morning I took the girls to school as normal. I deliberately kept myself busy all day, trying to avoid thinking about what was going to happen later that afternoon. Louisa had come home early from work so she was there when Lizzie and Joe brought the girls round to say goodbye. I gave them their memory boxes, full of little things to remind them of their year with us.

'This is from Jasmine,' I said, handing them a present.

It was a framed photo of all five of us.

'Oh, that's lovely,' said Lizzie. 'You can put it in your bedroom, girls.'

Both of them gave the baby a gentle hug and a kiss.

'Now come here and give me a cuddle,' I said, handing Jasmine to Lizzie.

I knew from all my years of experience that big emotional goodbyes were no good for anyone, especially little ones. But it took enormous effort and concentration to stop myself from crying and to plaster a cheerful smile on my face as I said my final goodbye.

'Bye bye, darling,' I said to Polly, wrapping my arms around her and breathing in her familiar smell one last time. 'See you very soon.'

I did the same with Daisy. I savoured that last cuddle with both of them, closing my eyes and memorising the feel of them in my arms.

'Now, off you go to that lovely pink bedroom of yours,' I said, my voice quivering slightly as tears choked my throat. 'I'll pop in and see you soon.'

Lizzie must have noticed I was struggling to keep it together.

'Bye Maggie,' she said, giving me a hug. 'I hope you're OK.'

'I'll be absolutely fine,' I said, although I felt differently inside. 'You enjoy your new family.'

'Oh, we will,' she smiled, handing Jasmine back to me.

Louisa gave them both a cuddle and then we waved the car off. As we walked inside and closed the front door, Louisa burst into tears.

'Oh, lovey,' I said, giving her a hug, my own tears brimming.

'If I'd been older and had my own house I'd have adopted them,' she sobbed. 'I love those girls to bits.'

'I know you do,' I said. 'I do too, but look where they're going and think how happy they're going to be.'

I knew it upset her too when kids left. She got enormously attached to them and I sometimes felt incredibly guilty about that. I had chosen to have this life, knowing that it involved loving children and then letting them go. Over the years I'd had to do that many times, but Louisa hadn't. She was only young and I knew how hard and upsetting it was for her to say goodbye.

'Well, that's that,' she sighed. 'I hate it when they go. You don't mind if I go round to Charlie's, do you, Maggie? He said he'd take me to Nando's to cheer me up.'

'Not at all,' I replied. 'You go off and enjoy yourself.'

I quite liked having a bit of time on my own to reflect. I decided to give Graham a quick call.

'The twins have gone,' I told him sadly.

'Oh, Maggie, that must have been hard,' he told me. 'I know you were really attached to them.'

'How are you feeling?'

'A bit flat and teary, to be honest,' I sighed. 'But I'll be OK. I always am.'

'I don't know how you do it,' he said, gently.

'You just have to,' I replied. 'You have to get on with it.'

It was nice to catch up with Graham and share our news with one another.

'Well, you take care of yourself,' he said, after we'd chatted for ten minutes.

'I will,' I reassured him. 'I've got a lovely little baby here keeping me company too, so I can't feel too sorry for myself.'

Jasmine was a welcome distraction from missing the twins and that afternoon she got a lot more snuggles and kisses.

'Hopefully it will be your turn soon, little missy, and we'll have to say bye bye to you,' I sighed as I put her to bed that night.

Again, the idea of her leaving brought up mixed emotions. I'd be delighted if things worked out for Hailey, but I'd so miss my cuddles with her baby.

After I'd put Jasmine down in her cot, I found myself wandering into the twins' room. I made a mental note to stop calling it that now, as it didn't help any of us to move on.

When I was feeling sad I always found keeping busy helped so I got to work. I stripped the girls' beds and moved them around so that the room looked a bit different, then I collected the few toys that were left and put them in a box.

Tomorrow I was on a mission to go to the DIY shop and choose some new paint. Again, redecorating when a child left after a long period of time was part of the healing process for me and I found it very therapeutic. In my heart, though, I knew it would take a long time for my sadness to fade.

The one good thing about the twins leaving was that now I could focus solely on Jasmine and Hailey. I knew it was going to be a tough time for Hailey as Martin was due to appear in court to be sentenced and her assessment was drawing to an end. The next few weeks were going to determine the rest of her life.

I didn't want to keep going on about the sentencing, but Hailey was actually the one who brought it up one morning when she was over to see Jasmine.

'Maggie, I've made a decision about the sentencing,' she told me. 'I've been talking to my police liaison officer and I've decided I want to go to court. I want to see Martin.'

My heart sank. Surely she wasn't still having thoughts about getting back together with him? Hailey must have seen my face and known what I was thinking.

'I'm not thinking about going back to him,' she said quickly. 'Honestly, Maggie, I'm not. I want to see him and show him that I'm stronger now. I want him to know Jasmine and I are living our lives just fine without him.'

I wasn't sure it was a good idea. Who knew how Hailey would react in a court room seeing Martin for the first time since he'd attacked her. It might do her more harm than good.

'Maggie, will you come with me to court?' she asked.

'Yes, if you really want me to, then of course I will,' I said. 'However, I do think you need to talk to Claire about this.'

'It's nothing to do with Claire,' she replied. 'If I want to go then she can't stop me.'

'You're right,' I said. 'But I still think it's a good idea to chat it through with her.'

'Would you ask her for me?' Hailey asked, suddenly shy.

I agreed and that afternoon gave Claire a ring.

'She seems very determined to go, although I'm not convinced,' I said, after bringing her up to speed. 'What do you think?'

'If it's important to her then I don't see why not,' Claire replied. 'Maybe seeing him is her way of saying goodbye and getting some closure. It will also be a public acknowledgement that what he did to her was wrong – and that might help. And you'll be with her to support her.'

I just hoped she was right.

As the day of the sentencing drew closer, I thought Hailey might change her mind. But she didn't.

I was still worried about how she was going to react. She sounded very strong and defiant, but when she actually saw Martin in the flesh there was a chance she might go to pieces.

I really felt quite nervous about it all. Hailey was doing so well lately and I didn't want this to set her back. But I knew the decision was hers.

'I got in touch with my police liaison officer today and told her I wanted to come,' Hailey told me. 'She said we could come into court through a special entrance so there was no chance of me bumping into Martin. She's going to make sure there's space in the public gallery for us to sit there.'

'Hailey, you don't have to do this, you know,' I told her. 'You can change your mind.'

'I want to,' she said emphatically. 'It's important for me and Jasmine. I need to see for myself what happens to him.'

On the morning of the sentencing, Vicky came round with her kids to look after Jasmine.

'Good luck,' she said. 'I hope it all goes OK.'

'So do I,' I sighed.

My stomach was churning. All I could hope was that Claire was right and that it gave Hailey the closure that she so desperately needed. When I picked Hailey up at the refuge I could tell she was terrified. She looked like she hadn't slept a wink and she was very quiet all the way to court.

'How are you feeling?' I asked her.

'Sick with nerves,' she replied. 'Nervous about seeing him again and what that will be like, and nervous that he'll get off or that he won't get a long sentence and will be out in a few months.'

The police had told us to expect a custodial sentence for such a serious assault and I prayed that they were right. I couldn't imagine what it would do to Hailey if he got off with anything less than that.

I pulled up into the car park of the crown court and turned my engine off. Hailey looked genuinely frightened as she looked around.

'Can you see him, Maggie?' she asked. 'Let me know if you see him. What happens if he notices me in court and tries to attack me?'

I put my hand on her shoulder in a bid to calm her down.

'Hailey, even if Martin sees you, he can't get to you,' I told her. 'He'll have guards either side of him so he can't get anywhere near you. He can't hurt you any more.'

'What if he starts shouting at me?' she asked, her eyes wide with fear.

'The judge won't allow that to happen. And if he does, he'll risk being in contempt of court.'

Hailey's police liaison officer, Hannah, was waiting for us at a side entrance to the court and took us inside.

'You can wait here,' she said, leading us down a corridor to a small room. 'It's normally where witnesses wait before they give evidence, but I don't want to risk you bumping into Martin outside the court.

'Hailey, the judge has got a copy of your victim impact statement and it's up to you whether you want to read it yourself in court or you want a member of the court staff to do it.'

This was the first time I'd heard anything about a victim impact statement and I wasn't aware Hailey had even done one.

'I'll do it,' she said. 'I want to read it myself.'

'Hailey, are you sure you're up to it?' I asked, concerned.

'I want to do it,' she replied. 'I want everyone to hear exactly what he has done to me and Jasmine.'

'If you change your mind during the sentencing hearing then I can let the court staff know,' Hannah told her.

It was a huge thing for Hailey to get up in court, in front of everyone, and talk about something so upsetting and personal. I was worried that when the time came it would all be too much for her. But there wasn't time to dwell on it. Soon it was time to go into court and take our places in the public gallery. It was a modern courtroom and even though it was one of the smaller ones, there was something about the hushed atmosphere and the barristers in their wigs and gowns that made it feel quite intimidating.

As Martin walked into the dock I felt Hailey stiffen next to me. She reached for my hand and squeezed it tightly.

'Take deep breaths,' I whispered to her. 'And remember he can't hurt you any more.'

Martin was dressed smartly in a suit and tie. But there were dark shadows under his eyes and he looked older somehow. We all stood when the judge came in and I noticed Martin glancing around the court room. When he looked over at us and saw Hailey he did a double take.

I suddenly realised how different she must have looked to him. One of the women at the refuge was a hairdresser and she had cut Hailey's long straggly hair into a bob and she'd started wearing a little bit of make-up. Louisa had lent her a green blouse that she wore with a pair of black trousers that Vicky had given her. She looked healthier, less pale, less frightened.

'What happens if he gets off with a slap on the wrist, Maggie?' she whispered. 'How am I going to cope?'

I prayed that he wouldn't.

The prosecutor read out the long list of Hailey's injuries, from her broken nose to her cracked ribs and internal bruising, as well as the older injuries that had been detected.

'This was a particularly vicious assault carried out on the defendant's wife in their own home. From the victim's medical records, we can see it's clearly not the first time that this has happened,' he told the judge.

'I have the pre-sentencing report and I believe there's also a victim impact statement. Your honour, I believe the victim would like to read out her statement herself.'

I could feel Hailey trembling next to me and she looked like she was about to pass out.

'You don't have to do this,' I told her. 'Just say the word and one of the court staff will do it.'

'No, I want to,' she said, standing up and walking towards the court clerk who led her to the witness box. She was offered a seat but she shook her head. She took a sip of water, cleared her throat and began to talk.

'I have lived in fear for most of my adult life because of the defendant's actions. I've endured years of hurt, humiliation and pain at his hands. On the night he attacked me I genuinely believed that I was going to die as he kicked me countless times in the head and body.'

Hailey's voice trembled at first but she spoke clearly and confidently. She looked straight at Martin but he sat in the dock with his head in his hands looking at the floor.

The coward.

'But the thing that has caused me the most pain in all of this is the fact that the defendant didn't allow me to be a proper mother to my daughter for the first four months of her life.

I wasn't allowed to pick her up, talk to her or play with her. I couldn't cuddle her when she was crying or feed her when she was hungry. That's something I still feel so guilty about and that I will regret for the rest of my life.'

She had managed to stay composed up until now but at the mention of Jasmine, Hailey's voice cracked with emotion.

With shaking hands, she took another sip of water.

'Do you wish to continue?' the judge asked her. 'The prosecutor can read the rest for you if don't feel you can manage to go on.'

Hailey shook her head defiantly.

'No, I'm fine,' she said.

She took a deep breath and continued.

'My little girl might not have been physically hurt by the defendant but she was mentally traumatised by being born into such a fearful, controlling and toxic environment. Since I have left the defendant, my child and I have flourished in ways I could never have imagined. My only regret is not doing it sooner.'

'Thank you for that, Mrs Henley,' the judge told her.

Hailey walked back to the gallery where she collapsed into my arms. Her shoulders shook as she sobbed silently into my shoulder.

'You were unbelievably brave and courageous to do that,' I whispered to her. 'I'm so, so proud of you. I couldn't believe the difference between the Hailey Henley who stood so defiantly in the witness box, and the Hailey Henley who couldn't meet my eye at that first meeting all those months ago.

'I just wanted the judge to hear it from me about what it was like,' she said.

'Well, I think it more than did the trick,' I replied, my heart swelling with pride. 'Do you want to go out for some fresh air?'

She shook her head.

The judge was about to pass sentence and Martin stood up in the dock.

'Martin Henley, you subjected your wife to a particularly nasty assault and as we heard from her, she feared for her own life.

'The seriousness of your crime warrants a custodial sentence.'

I held my breath. Hailey reached for my hand and squeezed it tightly.

Please make him pay.

'I sentence you to four years imprisonment.'

'Yes!' hissed Hailey victoriously next to me and I breathed out a huge sigh of relief.

Martin looked stunned and burst into tears.

As the guards took him away, he looked up at us in the public gallery.

'Hailey, I'm sorry,' he shouted. 'I love you.'

She stared at him but she didn't say a word. When he'd been led out, Hailey shook her head.

'He's pathetic. He's not crying for what he did to us, he's crying for himself. He's just a pathetic coward.'

As we came out of court, Hailey looked shell-shocked.

'How are you feeling?' I asked, enveloping her in a big hug.

'Happy, sad, sick, angry, pleased. I don't really know,' she laughed shakily.

I could see it had taken it out of her encountering Martin again, and she was exhausted.

'Are you glad you came?' I asked.

'Yes,' she said. 'I'm not frightened of him. He can't hurt me or Jasmine any more. He's just pathetic, Maggie.'

I could see she felt vindicated.

'Everyone believed me,' she said. 'They all know what he did to me was wrong, and they've punished him for it.'

'Well, I thought you were amazing in there,' I told her. 'You were so composed and strong. Every single person in that court was listening to you, and understood what you had gone through.'

I handed her my mobile.

'I think you should give Claire a ring and tell her the good news,' I said. 'It would be nice for her to hear it from you.'

'Claire, he got four years,' Hailey told her when she got through. Then she burst into tears and handed the phone back to me.

'How is she, Maggie?' asked Claire.

'A little bit overwhelmed,' I said. 'But I think they're tears of joy and absolute relief.'

'That's brilliant,' said Claire. 'I'm so pleased.'

Instead of heading straight home we walked to a nearby café for a celebration lunch.

'It's weird, but already I feel different,' said Hailey. 'I finally feel safe. I'm not looking over my shoulder any more.

'I'll be able to take Jasmine for a walk now and not be worried I'm going to bump into him. My life starts now, Maggie.'

And she was right. She had a future ahead of her at last.

NINETEEN

Moving On

Now the court case was over and Martin was safely locked away, Hailey could finally move on with her life. But when I next saw her she looked like she had the weight of the world on her shoulders.

'What is it?' I asked. 'What's happened?'

'I'm never going to get away from him, am I?' she sighed.

Hailey explained she'd had a phone call to say the house that she'd lived in with Martin was about to be cleared and put up for rent.

'I've still got my door keys so Liz at the refuge said I should use the opportunity to go back and get some of my things like my birth certificate and stuff.'

'Do you want to go back?' I asked her.

She shook her head.

'The thought of even walking in the front door makes me feel sick,' she continued. 'But I know she's right and it would probably be sensible to get some of my personal documents and it would save me time and money I'd spend sorting out new ones.

'There's also my grandma's jewellery box I'd love to have.

'But Maggie, if I went, would you please come with me?'

'Of course I will,' I said.

I knew it would be hard for her going back to a place that held so many bad memories for her, so the following day we put Jasmine in the car and drove back to her old neighbourhood. It was a nice area and she directed me to a row of pretty Victorian terraced houses overlooking a park.

'It's this one,' she said and I saw her visibly shudder as I pulled up outside.

'Are you sure you want to do this?' I asked her. 'I can drive away.'

'No, no, we're here now,' she said quickly.

Hailey was worried that Martin had changed the locks after she'd left. But her key still worked in the front door. I carried Jasmine as we stepped into the hallway. Everything looked very bare. It was freezing cold.

'I hate it,' she says. 'It brings back so many horrible memories being here.'

'It's so cold,' I shivered.

'It always was,' she sighed. 'Martin wouldn't let me put the heating on. I was relieved when Jasmine was due at the end of spring as I was so worried about her being cold.'

As we walked into the kitchen at the back of the house, Hailey gasped.

'Oh my God,' she sighed.

The sink was piled high with dirty dishes, there was rotting rubbish overflowing in the bin and there were cans of lager and pizza boxes littering every surface. The place was filthy and it stank.

'Was it always like this?' I asked.

Hailey shook her head.

'Martin made me keep it immaculate,' she said. 'I'd spend hours every day cleaning and scrubbing every surface until my knuckles bled.

'I can't believe he's left it like this. He was obviously cocky enough to think that he wasn't going to go to prison.'

The other rooms downstairs were in a similar state.

'I wasted so much of my life within these four walls,' she sighed. 'Everywhere I look reminds me of the times he hurt me. The dent in the living room wall is where he banged my head against it. The stain in the kitchen is where he threw his plate at me because his dinner wasn't warm enough, and it smashed on the door.

'And the last time I was here,' she said, her eyes filling with tears, 'I was lying on that floor in the hall terrified that I was going to die as he kicked me over and over again.'

'Oh, Hailey,' I sighed, putting my arm around her shoulders. 'You poor thing. You've been through so much.'

I started to think coming back here had been a bad idea, and I didn't want to traumatise her any more.

'You go upstairs and get what you need and then we can get out of here,' I told her. 'I'll go into Jasmine's room and start packing up her cot and anything else she might need.'

Hailey pointed me to Jasmine's room at the front of the house. It, too, was very bare. In the middle of the room was what looked like a cot, but it had been broken into bits. The mattress lay next to it. It had been slashed all over so the stuffing was seeping out. There was a bent and broken pushchair in the corner.

Hailey walked in and burst into tears.

'He's destroyed everything,' she sobbed. 'I don't care about the clothes because I hated them, but he's smashed up my grandma's jewellery box and cut up all my childhood photos.'

The only thing she'd managed to salvage was her birth certificate which she'd hidden in a drawer.

'I'm sorry, but he's trashed Jasmine's stuff too,' I told her. I couldn't believe the lengths that brute would go to.

'I don't care,' she said. 'I don't want her having these things anyway. I'll get her new stuff.'

She wandered over to the bedroom window and looked out across at the park.

'I used to stand here for ages watching all the mums playing with their babies, and I'd just cry that I wasn't allowed to take my daughter out and be like them.

'I wasn't even allowed to push her pram down the street on my own. Martin was always there, watching, threatening.

'I just hope that Jasmine's too young to remember any of it,' she said, ruffling her daughter's blonde hair. Jasmine looked up at her with wide-eyed innocence.

'Come on,' I told her. 'Let's get out of here.'

I carried Jasmine downstairs, opened the front door and went outside. Hailey hung back and looked around wistfully.

'I never want to think about this place again,' she said. 'It just reminds me of him.'

'You don't have to any more,' I replied. 'That chapter of your life is over.'

Hailey closed the door and posted the keys through the letterbox.

I could see she was really shaken and she sat in the car looking pensive. I put my hand on hers.

'What is it?' I said.

'Maggie, can the judge change his mind?' she asked. 'Can he say he's made a mistake and let Martin go?'

I shook my head.

'Martin is safely locked away in prison. He can't hurt you,' I told her. 'He can try and appeal against his sentence, but the likelihood is that won't happen.

'He's going to be in there for a long, long time and if anything changes the police will let you know.'

Even though Hailey had been to court and seen it for herself she still didn't truly believe that she was safe.

'There are things that you can do if it would help you feel more secure,' I told her. 'You can revert back to your maiden name or you can even change your name completely. We can look at all the options.'

I knew it would take a long time until she finally felt free of the prison he'd made for her.

A couple of days later Hailey had some good news to share with me.

'I got a letter today offering me a house!' she grinned.

She told me Social Services had written to the council in support of her application, and Liz at the refuge had helped her to fill out all the forms.

'I can't believe I'm going to have a place of my own,' she said. 'And it's two-bedroom. That's a good sign, isn't it, that Social Services want me to have a two-bedroom place? That means Jasmine can have her own room if she comes to live with me.'

'It sounds perfect,' I told her.

The housing association had said she could go and look at it the following day.

'I know it sounds silly, Maggie, but I'd really like Jasmine to come with me. I know she's just a baby but I'm hoping she'll be living there too, so I really want her to see it. Would you be able to bring her and come with me? I've asked Claire and she said she's fine with it.'

I could see how excited she was and I knew this was really special for her. If all went well, it was going to be her first home with Jasmine.

'Would you like me to pick you up to save you getting the bus over?'

'Yes, please,' she smiled.

The following day, the three of us drove over there. It was in an area neither of us knew, around half an hour from my house.

I think it was a comfort for Hailey that it was nowhere near where she had lived with Martin.

We pulled up outside the house, on a newly built estate. It was a small two-up, two-down and was immaculate inside. It was the complete opposite to the house she'd shared with Martin – it was light and bright, everything gleaming and brand new.

'Wow,' sighed Hailey, looking amazed. 'I absolutely love it.' She couldn't wipe the smile off her face.

'It's perfect,' I agreed, my face mirroring hers.

There were two bedrooms and a bathroom upstairs, a lounge and a little kitchen downstairs. There was even a small back garden with a shed.

'Jasmine is going to love playing out here,' she added.

Hailey had been told she could move in within the week.

'I bet you'll be glad to leave the refuge,' I said.

'I've kind of got used to it,' she replied. 'In a way I'll miss it. The staff are lovely and some of the women have been really nice to me. I'll never be one for big groups, but it will be strange and very quiet being on my own again.'

This was more change for her to cope with, but it was such a positive change. This was her first home where hopefully she and her baby could build a life and a future together.

Although Hailey's assessment was going well, she and I both knew that there were no guarantees that Jasmine would be able to go back and live with her.

'It's not a foregone conclusion, so I don't want to get your hopes up,' I said. 'Sometimes Social Services might extend an assessment if they're not sure or feel they need more time.'

'I know,' she sighed. 'I'm trying to keep positive but I'm scared, Maggie.'

A review meeting was to be held at my house in three days, around the time her assessment was due to come to an end.

'Do you think they'll tell me then?' Hailey asked.

'I think so, yes. My guess is that they'll probably know what they're intending to do,' I told her.

As the day of the review drew closer Hailey was a nervous wreck. She was hardly sleeping and very weepy.

'What if they don't think I'm strong enough to look after Jasmine?' she sobbed. 'What if they're still not convinced I'm not going to get back with Martin?'

'Hailey, you're working yourself up into a frenzy,' I told her. 'I don't honestly know what they're going to say but there's nothing you can do now to change it. You have to remain calm, for your sake and Jasmine's.'

'I don't think I could cope if I didn't get her back,' sobbed Hailey. 'It would kill me.'

'Stay positive, Hailey. That's all you can do,' I told her, trying my best to reassure her. I don't think it worked, though.

On the day of the review everyone was coming to my house – Claire, Neil and Hailey. We'd organised the meeting at the time Jasmine had her lunchtime sleep.

Hailey sat next to me, nervously picking at the skin around her fingernails.

'It's going to be OK,' I told her, squeezing her hand.

All I could do was hope beyond hope that they had come to the right decision. Hailey had been through so much but she was strong and she had fought for her daughter in the end. My overwhelming feeling was that she and Jasmine should be allowed to make a life together.

As the IRO, Neil was chairing the meeting.

'Hailey, it's obvious to all of us here that you love your daughter very much and she means the world to you,' he said.

'Yes, she does,' agreed Hailey, her voice shaking with nerves.

She looked like she was about to burst into tears.

'I just wanted to tell you how pleased I am personally to see you here today,' he told her. 'You look like a different person to when I last saw you all those months ago at Social Services. You're healthy, you're happy and you're confident – and most importantly you don't look scared any more.

'I know many of us here didn't think that things would work out like they have, but I'm genuinely delighted for you and I'm sorry for the horrendous things that your husband put you through. No one should suffer that.'

Just tell her, I thought to myself. *Tell her your decision, for God's sake!* My nerves couldn't handle it any more.

'I've spoken at length to Claire and to Jan, the contact worker, and Maggie, of course, and every single one of us agreed that you've proved that you're a great mum.'

'Everyone is so pleased with how you've done in your assessment and there has been nothing that has raised any concerns.'

He paused. Hailey looked like she was about to be sick.

I looked down at the floor and willed with every bone in my body that he was about to do the right thing.

'So I'm delighted to tell you that we'll be making the recommendation to the courts that Jasmine is returned to your care.'

'Really?' gasped Hailey, barely able to remain in her seat. 'Jasmine can live with me all the time?'

'Absolutely,' nodded Neil. 'You should be commended for your dedication to your daughter. You've had some challenges but you've stuck with it and you've demonstrated to us that your daughter is the most important person in your life.

'Congratulations,' he continued. 'I wish you and your little girl all the best for the future.'

Hailey jumped up to hug me, before collapsing into my arms with a huge sob. But they were tears of happiness and relief. I felt so proud of her. She deserved Neil's praise. I felt tears prick my own eyes as I held Hailey up.

'I can't believe it,' she gasped. 'I never thought it would happen.'

'Well done,' I told her, squeezing her tighter. 'You deserve it after everything you've been through.'

'Does that mean that's it, that I have full custody?' Hailey asked. 'There'll be no more Social Services involvement?'

'It means we'll ask the court to turn the care order into a supervision order,' Claire explained to her. 'Social Services still want to keep a close eye on things. It will be a three-month supervision order and I'll still be Jasmine's social worker so I'll pop in from time to time to check you're both OK.'

'Check up on me you mean?' sighed Hailey.

'Not at all,' said Claire. 'I'll be there to support you with anything you need help with. We don't want you to feel like you've just been abandoned.'

'But the supervision order still means that Jasmine can come and live with me?' Hailey asked again, suddenly unsure of herself.

'Yes, your daughter can come and live with you,' smiled Neil. 'Hailey, none of us have any concerns about your ability to be Jasmine's mum.'

The tears made way for a great big grin on her face.

I made everyone a cup of tea and got out the sponge cake I'd made the day before with *Well done Hailey* iced on the top.

'How could you have been so sure?' Hailey said when she saw it. 'I wasn't.'

'I was hoping that you'd get the right outcome,' I said. 'I wanted to do something nice for you because you have worked so hard to get your life back together.

'How do you feel?' I asked her.

'Oh, Maggie, I'm so, so chuffed,' she said. 'I can't wait for Jasmine to wake up now so I can take her back to the refuge.

'Would you mind giving us a lift, Maggie?'

I could see the excitement in her face and I hated having to be the one to burst her bubble.

'I'm so sorry, lovey, but it doesn't work like that,' I said. 'We have to sit down with Claire and talk about how we're going to do this.

'I know you want her back as soon as you can, but we've got to think about Jasmine and her needs. We'll settle her back in with you gradually just like we did with the twins, and it probably won't be for a few days yet.'

Hailey's face fell.

'But Jasmine's not being adopted,' she said. 'She knows me, I'm her mum.'

'I know you are, sweetie, but she hasn't lived with you for the past five months,' I said. 'If you take her back to the refuge tonight there will be nothing familiar around her and she will be completely thrown. If she's distressed, that will upset you.'

I knew Hailey understood all this but she was desperate to get her daughter back.

'But Maggie, I just can't wait for us to be a family.'

'We'll talk to Claire, but it makes sense to wait until you move into your new house next week. Then we can make sure you have everything you need for Jasmine to come home.

'You've got the rest of your lives to be a family.'

I could see Hailey was devastated

'I'm fed up of waiting,' she sobbed. 'I just want her back with me. I've got that cot in my room at the refuge so she's got somewhere to sleep. It would be fine.'

'I know you do, sweetie, but for both your sakes we want to make sure it's as smooth and easy as possible.'

Hailey was upset, but I knew in time she would understand that this was the best thing for Jasmine.

A few minutes later, crying echoed from the baby monitor and Hailey jumped up.

'Can I go and get her?' she asked.

'Of course you can,' I said.

It had been an emotional morning for her and I knew she could do with a cuddle.

On the monitor I heard her go into Jasmine's bedroom.

'Hello my gorgeous girl,' she cooed. 'Oh, I love you so, so much. And I've got some amazing news for you. You're coming back to live with Mummy. It's going to be very soon my princess, I promise.

'I'm the luckiest mummy in the whole world.'

As I heard her talking to her daughter I was filled with an overwhelming sense of relief. Jasmine was finally going back where she belonged.

Then I remembered that it also meant it was time for me to say another goodbye. I wasn't sure my heart could stand it.

TWENTY

Endings and Beginnings

As we pulled up into Joe and Lizzie's driveway, I could see Polly and Daisy jumping up and down and waving at the front window.

'I think it's safe to say they're excited to see us,' laughed Louisa.

The girls had been gone three weeks now and Joe and Lizzie had invited us to pop in for a cup of tea.

I got Jasmine out of her car seat in the back while Joe opened the front door. The twins rushed out to meet us and threw themselves into our arms.

'We missed you,' they said in unison.

'We missed you too,' I told them. 'It's so lovely to see you both.'

When they saw Jasmine they covered her in kisses and cuddles too.

'Thanks for coming round,' said Lizzie, leading us through to the living room. She looked a lot more tired than the last time I'd seen her.

We all sat down and had a cup of tea and the twins told us about school and the cat and how they were learning how to ride bikes.

'Guess what, girls?' I said. 'We had some good news the other day. Jasmine's going back to live with her mummy next week.'

'That's wonderful,' smiled Lizzie.

'Yes it really is,' I said.

The twins were desperate to give us a tour of their new house.

'Come and see our bedroom, Louisa,' said Polly. 'Everything is pink.'

'OK,' Louisa giggled as they dragged her upstairs.

'I'll come and look at it later, girls,' I called after them. I wanted to take the opportunity to have a chat in private with Lizzie and Joe and see how they were. I put Jasmine down on the carpet so she could have a crawl around.

'The twins seem really happy and settled,' I said. 'How are you both finding it?'

Joe and Lizzie looked at each other.

'It might look like happy families but believe me it isn't,' said Joe. 'It's been really tough, Maggie.

'We'll get through it but when you told us to be prepared, we really weren't.'

They described the problems they'd been having with the girls. Polly had regressed with her toilet training and had been having three or four accidents a day at school.

'But we haven't made a big deal of it and the school have been brilliant,' said Lizzie. 'Thankfully it seems to be getting better now.'

They'd also had issues with Daisy at bedtime. She'd been refusing to get into her pyjamas and then wouldn't stay in bed.

'It's taking hours just to get her to bed and she's been lashing out at me,' said Lizzie. 'She's been hitting and kicking me and the other day she bit me.

'She's fine with Joe. It just seems to be me.'

'Don't take it personally,' I said. 'She was like that when the girls first came to me. She's just feeling insecure about the changes and testing out the boundaries.'

Often when children are first adopted, they'll regress to the behaviours they're familiar with. Everything has changed in their little world so they go back to what they know best. This can, of course, send their new adoptive parents into a bit of a panic. In reality, it is part of building a bond of attachment to their new carers. It is almost as if they have to get that out of the way before they can attach.

It was what I had suspected might happen but it was good to see that Lizzie and Joe were staying calm and doing their best to deal with it.

'I know it's hard but honestly, it will pass,' I tried to reassure them. I just hoped that Jasmine's settling in was going to go a lot more smoothly.

The following day I helped Hailey move from the refuge into her new house.

When I went to pick her up, she was so excited. She still didn't have much stuff to pack. I'd lent her a case to put her clothes in and there were a few photos, a rug and a lamp to take.

'I've got the keys,' she smiled, jangling them in the air. 'I can't wait to get in there.'

Happily she loved it as much as she had the first time.

'I honestly can't believe my luck, Maggie,' she said. 'I can't believe that in less than a week Jasmine will be here with me too.'

'You'll be all settled and ready for her by then,' I said.

The refuge had helped her get a second-hand table and chairs, a sofa and a bed. Social Services had got Jasmine a cot. I was going to give her Jasmine's buggy and high chair and I'd got her some bedding and towels. It still looked quite bare and sparse but Hailey was excited about going shopping for a few knick-knacks to make it more homely.

Because the house was newly built, everything was brand new and sparkling. All it needed was a quick wipe down to get rid of the dust. Before I left I nipped to the car and got the spider plant and *Welcome to your new home* card I'd bought Hailey.

'Thank you, Maggie, it's lovely,' she sighed happily.

'I know you and Jasmine are going to be really happy here together,' I said.

Claire and I had worked out a plan of action to settle Jasmine back in with Hailey.

'I think three or four days will be fine,' said Claire. 'It's just to make sure Hailey feels confident and Jasmine seems settled.'

On the first day Hailey came over to my house to see Jasmine.

'I thought you might want to take her out for walk,' I told her.

'What?' she gasped. 'On my own?'

I looked at her and laughed.

'Hailey, in a few days you're going to be totally on your own with Jasmine all the time, so you'd better get used to it.'

For the past five months she hadn't been allowed to be on her own with her daughter, so it must have felt strange. I knew that in the past she'd always had Martin breathing down her neck.

She was surprisingly nervous and needed lots of reassurance.

'Maggie, please can you check I've fastened the harness right?' she asked. 'And I know she's got her snowsuit on but do you think she'll need a blanket as well? Will she get cold?'

'What do you think?' I asked her. 'You're her mummy.'

'I think I'll take a blanket just in case,' she said.

'There you go then,' I smiled.

It was about giving her the confidence to know that she could make those decisions for herself.

'I was sorting out a few finances last night and I worked out that Jasmine has over fifty pounds in pocket money,' I told her.

Every week, children in my care were given three pounds per week in pocket money from Social Services. As Jasmine was only a baby and I already had lots of books and toys, I'd saved hers and put it into a money box for her.

'I thought perhaps you might like to take her shopping and buy her some things she needs for the new house.'

'Oh yes, I'd love that,' she said.

Hailey came back a couple of hours later with lots of bags hanging off the pushchair handles.

'How did it go?' I asked.

'I loved it,' she said. 'I got so many lovely things.'

She opened the bags and showed me her purchases. She'd got Jasmine some bibs and plastic bowls and cutlery. She'd bought her a little pink lamp for her room and a heart-shaped rug for the floor by the cot.

'And I couldn't resist this,' she beamed, opening a Mothercare bag and showing me a beautiful blue dress with a lacey collar.

'Isn't it gorgeous?' she said. 'Don't worry, I bought this with my own money.'

'It's adorable,' I said. 'She will look lovely in that.'

Hailey looked so happy and I remembered that was one of her wishes – to go shopping and choose a pretty dress for her daughter.

Jasmine was going to spend the following day at Hailey's house. When I dropped her off I brought over her blanket, toys and some of her bedding so she'd have familiar things around her.

'Remember, you're giving her tea tonight and I'll come and get her later,' I told Hailey. 'Ring me if you're having any problems.'

'We'll be fine, Maggie,' she said.

I could tell she couldn't wait to spend time with Jasmine in their new home.

I went back and started packing up Jasmine's clothes as she would be going to live with Hailey permanently the following day.

I pulled out one drawer and to my horror saw the tattered Babygros and sleepsuits that Martin had insisted Jasmine wear when she first came to live with me. Even the sight of them made me feel furious at the way Martin had treated Hailey and Jasmine and how he had made them suffer.

There was no way I would take those to Hailey. I didn't want her reminded of the threadbare second-hand clothes that she and her baby had been forced to wear.

I picked them up, marched downstairs and threw them straight into the bin outside.

Good riddance, I thought to myself, smiling with satisfaction.

I didn't mention it to Hailey when I went back later to pick up Jasmine. I wondered what kind of a day they'd had, but when I arrived everything looked under control. There were toys and books all over the floor and Jasmine seemed happy and content and was crawling round.

'Have you had a good day with Mummy?' I asked, picking her up.

'She has,' said Hailey. 'We had a play and a walk to the local park and she ate all her tea.'

'I'm not in rush so I'm happy to hang around a bit longer if you want to give her a bath,' I told her. 'I can drive her home in her pyjamas and put her straight to bed.'

'That would be brilliant,' Hailey replied.

The following day was Saturday, the day Jasmine was going to go and live with Hailey for good. As this was a little bit different to a normal adoption, Louisa and I were talking to Hailey about how we could say our goodbyes.

'Why don't you all come over here and we'll spend the day together,' suggested Hailey.

'We could help you paint Jasmine's bedroom,' Louisa suggested. She and Hailey had become good friends by now.

'That's a great idea,' I said.

I knew Hailey had been desperate to give Jasmine a pink girly bedroom ever since she'd heard me talk about the twins' new room.

'We can all take it in turns to look after Jasmine while the other two paint, and then I'll treat us all to a takeaway afterwards,' I said.

We had a great day and Jasmine's bedroom looked brilliant by the time we had finished, although we were all exhausted. Everything had seemed so normal and relaxed that it was only after we'd eaten our takeaway that it began to hit me why we were there and that Jasmine wasn't coming home with us. Hailey must have sensed how I was feeling and that I might like some time on my own with the baby.

'Maggie, I'm not trying to get out of it or anything, but I wondered if you wanted to give Jasmine her bath tonight?'

'Oh, yes, I'd love that,' I replied gratefully.

I took her upstairs and got her undressed on the change mat while the bath was running. Well, I tried to get her undressed. She kept wriggling around and flipping herself over and then crawling off.

'Oi, come here missy,' I laughed.

In the end I practically had to wrestle her to the ground to get her clothes off.

It struck me then how different she was to the stiff little baby who had arrived at my house five long months ago – the baby who wouldn't even make eye contact with me and who didn't utter a sound when I changed her nappy. All that was such a contrast to the chunky nine-month-old in front of me today, who couldn't keep still for a second.

Once I'd finally managed to get her undressed, I lifted Jasmine into the bath. She splashed and babbled away and played with the little plastic boats Hailey had got her. I chattered away to her too.

'Isn't it exciting. You're in your new bathroom in your new home. From tonight you're going to be with your mummy all the time. Isn't that wonderful?'

Jasmine grinned up at me and then splashed her hand down into the bath so I got drenched with water.

'You are very cheeky,' I smiled and she giggled and did the same thing all over again.

This was another goodbye and another chapter closing in my fostering life. As much as I was delighted for Hailey, another part of me was grieving for my own loss. I'd fallen in love with Jasmine and I was so sad to see her go.

She hadn't really been the issue at all in this placement. The key had been Hailey realising she was strong enough to come out of her abusive relationship. It had been about giving Hailey the confidence to stand on her own two feet and make the decision that her daughter was more important than anything, and I was so happy that she had done that in the end.

Once Jasmine was in her clean nappy and her sleepsuit, I carried her downstairs.

'All done,' I said.

'Do you want to put her to bed, Maggie, one last time?' asked Hailey.

'That would be lovely,' I said. 'You know me, I always take the opportunity to sneak in an extra cuddle where I can.'

I was making light of it but inside my heart was breaking at the realisation that I wasn't going to be seeing this little girl for a while.

Hailey and Louisa gave her a kiss and I took Jasmine upstairs. Rather than putting her straight down, I held her in my arms and walked around the room for a little while.

I kissed her on the head and whispered gently in her ear, breathing in her lovely baby scent.

'Goodnight little one. It's so hard to let you go but I know you're in the best place with your mummy.

'Be happy.'

I laid her down in her cot and she stared back at me with her big blue trusting eyes.

'I'm going to miss you so much,' I whispered then I walked out.

I stood at the top of the stairs and gulped back my tears before I went back down to see Hailey and Louisa.

'I think she'll be out like a light,' I told Hailey. 'She's very tired.'

Turning to Louisa, I said, 'And we'd better be heading off.'

She got up and gave Hailey a hug.

'See you very soon,' she told her.

Then it was my turn.

'You look after yourself and that gorgeous girl of yours,' I told her.

'I will,' she smiled, holding me tight. 'Thank you for everything, Maggie.'

'It was all down to you,' I said. 'You and Jasmine are here because of your bravery, courage and determination.'

'Were there times when you never thought you'd see this day happen?' she asked.

'Absolutely,' I said. 'You've had your wobbles but you worked through them, and look at you now. You're a totally different person. You're free, Hailey.'

'Now I'm here with Jasmine, I finally feel like that part of my life is over with,' she said. 'I don't want to waste another second thinking about that man and what he did to us.

'I've got my daughter back and that's all that matters.'

Her eyes filled up with tears. I wrapped my arms around her and gave her another big hug.

'Will you still see us?' she asked. 'I know you'll miss Jasmine but I'd like to see you too.'

'Of course I'll still see you if you want me to,' I said, smiling. 'You've got my number. I'd be delighted to see you both anytime, and I know you and Louisa will keep in touch. You're such a strong person, Hailey, and Jasmine is lucky to have a mummy like you. I'm going to miss you terribly.'

'Thank you,' she said. 'For everything.'

Louisa and I walked out to the car.

'Another goodbye,' she said. 'I'll be getting used to this.'

'You never get used it,' I sighed, my voice cracking with emotion.

Tears streamed down my face. I couldn't hold them back any longer.

'I wondered when you were going to cry,' said Louisa. 'You normally do.'

'Honestly, they're happy tears,' I sobbed. 'I'm so happy for Hailey, I'm just going to miss her and Jasmine so much.'

'I know you will,' said Louisa, giving my hand a squeeze. 'I'm going to miss her too.'

I got a huge sense of satisfaction when things worked out in my placements. It didn't always happen, but it was a nice feeling to know that I had done my best for a child and that she was happy.

My tears dried and I ended up quietly smiling to myself as I drove home.

'What are you thinking?' asked Louisa.

'Five months ago I would never have believed Jasmine and Hailey would be happy and safe and living in their own house and I'm genuinely delighted for them,' I said, and turned to Louisa. 'It doesn't mean to say I won't miss them terribly, but we have to focus on the positives.'

'You're right,' she sighed. 'But promise me there will be no more goodbyes for a while?'

'I promise,' I said.

On Sunday morning I called round to see Vicky.

'Last night I dropped Jasmine off with Hailey,' I told her. 'They seemed really settled.'

'That's brilliant news,' Vicky replied. 'She's such a strong young woman to have come through all that. You and I both know that so many women choose their violent partners over their children.'

Sadly, she was right. Hailey was in the minority. So many women were caught in that cycle of abuse. Even if there are people who can help them get out of it, for many women they're so entrenched in it they can't. It's more scary for them to come out of that familiar situation than to stay in it. I was so glad Hailey had kept to her promise that she wouldn't get back with Martin.

'So now you've got an empty house, are you going to ring Becky tomorrow and put yourself back on the available list?' asked Vicky.

'Do you know what, Vic?' I said. 'I'm not, because I've decided to have a little break first. I'm going to go on holiday.'

'Holiday?' she said, surprised. 'But you hardly ever go on holidays, Maggie.'

'I know,' I said. 'The most I normally manage is a few days in a caravan or a cottage by the sea when I've got children with me.'

It had been such a manic and emotional few months with the twins and Jasmine. Now everyone had gone, I felt like I needed a bit of time and space to get my head around everything that had happened.

'So where are you going to go?' she asked.

'I honestly don't care,' I laughed. 'As long as there's nice scenery and I can sit and read a book for a week. I'm letting Graham choose.'

I saw the glee in Vicky's face.

'Ahh, so you're going with Graham, are you?' she teased.

'Yes,' I said. 'I've been feeling a bit guilty that we haven't spent any time together the past few months. So we said we'd go away.'

'That's lovely,' said Vicky. 'So tell me, Maggie, do I need to go out and buy myself a hat? Am I hearing wedding bells here?'

I felt myself blushing and I threw a cushion at her.

'Don't be so ridiculous,' I laughed.

I knew Vicky so well that I didn't mind her teasing me. I did feel faintly ridiculous having a boyfriend at my age, but Graham was a nice man and I was looking forward to our week away.

I spent the next few days batch cooking and filling plastic containers so Louisa had meals for the week.

'You've got a spag bol for Monday,' I told her, 'a chicken stew for Tuesday; maybe you could get a pizza Wednesday.'

'Maggie, I'm twenty,' she laughed. 'I can cook for myself. Anyway I'll probably be at Charlie's most of the time and I said I'd pop into Hailey's one night.'

'It's really lovely that you two are friends,' I said.

'You need a break,' she told me. 'Don't worry about anyone else. Just go and relax and enjoy yourself.'

I knew she was right.

It had been an emotional, intense few months. Being a foster carer is 24/7 and sometimes if you don't get a break you can burn out. What was that saying Becky was always quoting at me? 'You can't pour from an empty cup.'

After a little holiday I'd come back refreshed and recharged ready for whatever challenge was waiting for me next. And to be honest, I couldn't wait.

Acknowledgements

Thank you to my children, Tess, Pete and Sam. You are such a big part of my fostering today but I had not met you when Jasmine, Hailey, Polly and Daisy came into my home. To my wide circle of fostering friends – you know who you are! Your support and your laughter are valued. To my friend Andrew B for your continued encouragement and care. Thanks also to Heather Bishop, who spent many hours listening and enabled this story to be told; to my literary agent Rowan Lawton; and to Anna Valentine at Trapeze for giving me the opportunity to share these stories.

A Note from Maggie

I really hope you enjoyed reading Polly, Daisy, Jasmine and Hailey's stories. I love sharing my experiences of fostering with you, and I also love hearing what you think about them. If you enjoyed this book, or any of my others, please think about leaving a review online. I know other readers really benefit from your thoughts, and I do too.

To be the first to hear about my new books, you can keep in touch on my Facebook page @MaggieHartleyAuthor. I find it inspiring to learn about your own experiences of fostering and adoption, and to read your comments and reviews.

Finally, thank you so much for choosing to read *Battered, Broken, Healed*. If you enjoyed it, there are others available, including *Too Scared to Cry, Tiny Prisoners, The Little Ghost Girl, A Family for Christmas, Too Young to be a Mum, Who Will Love Me Now? The Girl No One Wanted, Sold to be a Wife* and *Is It My Fault Mummy?*. I hope you'll enjoy my next story just as much.

Maggie Hartley

Exclusive Sample Chapter

If you enjoyed *Battered, Broken, Healed,* read on for the first chapter of my book *Who Will Love Me Now*?, out now!

ONE

On the Cards

The woman carefully shuffled the pack of cards and fanned them out, face down, in front of me.

'Pick seven,' she told me.

After I'd done as she'd asked, she put the cards I'd chosen back down on the table and turned them over one by one.

She smiled.

'What is it?' I asked. 'What can you see?'

'Ooh, lots of things,' she said. 'What would you like to ask me, my dear?'

To be honest, I wasn't sure, as I'd never done this before. My friend Vicky, who was also a foster carer, had convinced me that having a tarot card reading at home one morning would be a bit of fun.

'Marjorie's meant to be really good,' she'd told me. 'My sister-in-law swears by her. She sees her every six months.'

I thought it was all mumbo jumbo but she'd persuaded me and so here we were. Vicky was in the kitchen, waiting to have her reading after mine. I don't know what I was expecting but Marjorie was an ordinary-looking lady in her fifties. It was hard to believe that this woman in jeans, a jumper and fake UGG boots could predict my future, but I was willing to give it a go.

'I've got a question for you,' I said. 'When will I be getting more children to foster?'

Marjorie picked up the first card, which had a picture of a king holding a gold disc on it.

'Ah, this suit of the tarot cards is all about your work and I can see that you love what you do very much,' she said. 'In fact, it's more of a vocation than a job for you. The good news is the cards are telling me that a new child will be arriving soon.'

'Ooh, how soon?' I asked.

'The cards are saying that there's a child on the way to you as we speak.'

'Really?' I gasped. 'Right now?'

Marjorie nodded.

'Is it a girl or a boy?' I asked. 'How old are they?'

'That, I'm afraid, I don't know,' she said. 'But if the cards are right then it won't be long before you find out.'

There were no other surprise revelations in the rest of my reading but I was excited at the possibility that I might be getting a new foster placement.

'What did she say?' Vicky asked when I went to get her from the kitchen for her reading.

'Well, I'm not going to win the lottery or meet the man of my dreams, but apparently there's a new foster placement on its way to me right now.'

'That's brilliant news,' she said.

I'd been on the available list with my fostering agency for the past couple of weeks but, so far, nothing had come up.

'I hope she's right,' I told Vicky. 'I'm ready for a new challenge.'

At that time I had two children living with me. Louisa had been with me since her parents had been tragically killed in a car crash five years ago. Alone and struggling to cope with her grief, she'd been painfully shy at first but she had turned into a strong, confident, determined young woman who I was very proud of. She'd recently turned eighteen so she was now an adult and officially out of the care system. Even though I wasn't legally fostering her any more, she would always be part of my family and she knew she could live with me for as long as she wanted to. She had finished a course in childcare and had just got a job as a nanny for a local family, which she was really enjoying.

Then there was baby Ryan, who was upstairs having his morning nap. He was six months old now and had been with me since he was two weeks old when his teenage parents had taken him to hospital, saying that he'd rolled off the sofa and bumped his head. Staff had been suspicious of this explanation as a baby that young doesn't roll and X-rays had shown he'd also got a fractured rib. An emergency protection order had been issued and he'd immediately been taken into care. The Crown Prosecution Service was still looking into whether there was enough evidence to charge his parents with hurting him. The plan was that Ryan would eventually go for adoption and I was looking after him until then. I had leapt at the chance to care for Ryan. It was heartbreaking to think that a tiny baby had gone through such pain and cruelty at the hands of the two people who were supposed to love him the most. It wasn't hard to get attached to babies and Ryan was a lovely smiley little boy. He had a lovely thick mop of blond curls and bright blue eyes that made him look like a little cherub. Thankfully, so far he didn't seem to have been affected by the traumatic start that he'd had to his life.

You might think that I had my hands full with a teenager and a young baby to look after, but the truth was, life was a bit too quiet for me. Louisa was at work all day or out with her friends and Ryan was an easy baby. I liked the noise and the chaos of having several children living with me and I had plenty of room in my six-bed house. My other long-term foster placement, Lily, had gone back to live with her birth mother several months ago and I'd said goodbye to teenage mum Jess and her baby Jimmy around the same time, as they now had their own place along with Jimmy's dad Darren. Since they'd all left I'd had a few respite placements but now I was hoping for something a bit more long term.

Although I always liked the challenge of stroppy teenagers, my ideal was a child or children under twelve. I found that age group particularly interesting – I liked the endless questions, the funny things they said and the way their minds were like little sponges soaking up everything around them.

Yep, life is a bit too quiet and organised for me at the minute, I thought as I flicked the kettle on to make everyone a cup of tea.

I was putting some digestive biscuits onto a plate when my mobile rang. I recognised the number flashing up on the screen – it was Becky, my supervising social worker from the fostering agency I worked for. She'd been my link worker ever since I'd joined the agency well over a year ago and we got on really well.

'Hi, Maggie,' she said. 'I'm not disturbing anything, am I?'

'If I told you what was going on at my house at the minute you'd think I was mad.' I smiled, thinking about the tarot card reader in the front room. 'What can I do for you?'

'I've just had a call from a social worker called Kate Lewis who said she'd worked with you in the past.'

She was at the local authority that I'd worked for before I'd moved to the agency. She'd been the social worker on a couple of placements I'd had way back when I'd first started fostering. I remembered Kate because she was very well spoken and was always perfectly turned out, with swishy hair and expensive-looking clothes.

The cases we'd worked on together had been two troubled teens – one of them had threatened me with a gun and the other was a persistent runaway, so they had both been a challenge, to say the least.

'Gosh that was years ago,' I told Becky. 'I'm surprised she remembers me.'

'Well, you must have made an impression as she asked for you specifically,' she replied. 'She needs someone to take an emergency placement and she said you were good with tricky cases.'

'Ah, it's one of those, is it?' I asked, wondering exactly what 'tricky' meant in this situation. 'Have you got any more details about the child or how long they're likely to be with me?'

'All I know is that it's a ten-year-old girl and Kate needs an answer ASAP as she has to be placed today.'

Sometimes in fostering, especially when it's an emergency placement, you have to make a decision based on only the scantest of information.

'OK,' I said. 'Tell Kate I'll take her.'

I'd been hoping for a child under twelve and because Kate had asked for me personally I felt obliged to help.

'Either Kate or I will be in touch when we know more about when she'll be arriving,' she said.

'No problem,' I said. 'Speak soon.'

As I hung up, Vicky came into the kitchen with Marjorie, the tarot card reader.

'You won't believe this, but that was my link worker from the fostering agency offering me a new placement,' I told them. 'It's a little girl. She's coming today.'

'You see,' said Marjorie. 'The cards are never wrong.'

She left with a big smile on her face, clearly delighted that one of her predictions had come true. Ryan was still asleep so Vicky stuck around for a cup of tea and a chat.

'Do you need a hand getting the bedroom ready?' she asked me.

'I don't think there's much to do,' I said. 'I'll probably put her in Lily's old room.'

I'd recently done a respite placement for a weekend for three siblings so there were bunk beds in there now, as well as a single bed.

'Do you think I should take the bunks down?' I asked Vicky. 'There's more room in there when it's just a single.'

'I'd leave it until you know a bit more about her,' she said.

She was right. For all I knew, the girl might only be with me for a few days, depending on the circumstances.

'I'll be off now, so you can get ready for your new arrival,' said Vicky. 'As the cards predicted.'

'A coincidence, if you ask me.' I smiled. 'I'm still not sure I believe in all that and, besides, it's not exactly a surprise when I've been on the vacant list for weeks.'

When Vicky had gone, I woke Ryan up from his nap and began making his lunch. He was such a happy boy and even though I'd disturbed him from a deep sleep, he grinned up at me with his big blue eyes. Ryan was used to having all my attention when Louisa was at work and I hoped the little girl who was on her way to us liked babies and would grow to love him as much as I did. He'd recently started on solids so I was busy mashing some carrot and swede up for him when my phone went.

'Hi, Kate, it's nice to hear from you after all these years,' I said, recognising the well-spoken voice on the other end of the line. 'My link worker Becky said you'd be calling.'

'Yes,' she said. 'I've got a case I thought you might be able to help with. It's a ten-year-old girl called Kirsty.'

'Becky said it was an emergency placement so I'm assuming she's about to be taken into care today?' I asked.

'Actually, she's already in care,' Kate explained. 'She's been fostered long term by the same couple since she was a toddler.'

'Oh, I see,' I said, surprised.

This case was getting more intriguing, and confusing, by the minute.

'I haven't got huge amounts of time to fill you in now but the gist of it is that Kirsty's lived with Pat and Mike since she was nine months old.

'This morning she was at home with Pat when she collapsed. Kirsty rang Social Services as she wasn't sure what to do and found the number on Pat's phone.

'One of my colleagues phoned an ambulance and Pat was rushed to hospital.'

'Oh no,' I said. 'That's terrible. How is she?'

'All I know is that the doctors think it was a heart attack and Mike is up at the hospital with her now.

'They're obviously both very shocked so we need someone to look after Kirsty until we know what Pat's prognosis is and what's happening.'

'The poor girl,' I said.

It must have been terrifying for her to see her foster mother keel over like that in front of her and then be rushed off in an ambulance.

While Kate was explaining all this to me, I could hear someone shouting and carrying on in the background.

'Who on earth's that?' I asked.

'That's Kirsty,' she told me. 'She's a bit – how can I put this? – lively.

'Would you mind having a quick word with her, Maggie? She's insisting that she talks to you.'

'I wanna speak to her,' I heard a voice say. 'Gimme the phone.'

'Here you go,' I heard Kate say.

'Hello, is that Kirsty?' I asked. 'I'm Maggie. I hear you're coming to stay with me while your foster mum's in hospital.'

'Yeah,' she said. 'Have you got any pets? I love animals, especially dogs, which I love more than cats.

'Will I have my own bedroom? I hope so. And will there be lots of toys for me to play with? I love toys.'

She hardly paused for breath as she fired off one question after another without giving me the time to answer. She certainly wasn't the traumatised, scared little girl that I had expected. She sounded excited, like she was going on a holiday or a big adventure.

'I've got two cats called Billy and Mog,' I told her when I finally managed to get a word in edgeways.

'Oh,' she said. 'Well, I suppose I'll get used to them. I like rabbits too. Have you got any rabbits? I also like hamsters and gerbils but not mice. Don't like their tails.'

'Kirsty, please give me the phone back now. I need to speak to Maggie,' I heard Kate say.

She must have managed to grab her mobile off her as she finally came back on the line.

'Hi, Maggie. Sorry about that,' she said.

'Well that was, erm, interesting,' I said. 'She certainly sounds lively. Isn't she at all upset by what happened today?'

'Apparently not,' sighed Kate.

It was all very odd. However, I'd been doing this job long enough to know that trauma and shock could manifest themselves in lots of different ways. Kids often reacted entirely differently from how you expected them to.

Kate explained that she was helping Kirsty to get some of her things together.

'She's not being that helpful at the minute,' she told me quietly. 'But hopefully we'll be with you in an hour or so.'

'That's no problem,' I said. 'I'm in for the rest of the day so turn up whenever. I'm sure Becky gave you my address.'

In fact, it was a whole three hours later when the doorbell rang at just after 4 p.m. I picked up Ryan and went to answer it.

It was a freezing cold January day so it was already dark outside as I opened the door. On the doorstep was an extremely harassed-looking Kate. She was exactly as I'd remembered her – albeit slightly older and a bit more dishevelled. Standing next to her was a chubby little girl with long light brown wavy hair, dressed in leggings and a jumper, with a smug look on her face.

'Sorry we're late,' said Kate, giving me a weary smile. 'Things took slightly longer than I was anticipating.'

'No problem,' I told her.

'And you must be Kirsty,' I said, turning to the little girl. 'It's nice to meet you.'

She grinned at me.

'Oh, you've got a baby!' she yelled as she saw Ryan wriggling around in my arms. 'I love babies. Can I hold him?'

I hung onto him for dear life as she tried to grab him from me.

'That's probably not a good idea, lovey,' I told her gently. 'He's a lot heavier than he looks. Why don't you come in and let him get used to you first and then perhaps you can have a cuddle later on.

'Would you like a drink or anything to eat?' I asked as they came into the hallway.

'No thanks,' said Kirsty. 'Kate bought me an ice cream on the way here.'

'An ice cream?' I questioned, surprised.

It was a chilly winter's day, not exactly traditional ice cream weather.

'I had to stop and get her one,' Kate muttered, rolling her eyes. 'It was the only way I could persuade her to get in the car with me.'

I could tell that Kate had had a long, exhausting battle getting this child to my house. Kirsty, meanwhile, seemed full of energy and was as chirpy as she had been when I'd spoken to her on the phone earlier.

'Where's my room?' she asked. 'Can I see my room? I hope it's not pink. I hate pink. I can't sleep in a pink room. Are there any toys up there? I didn't bring any with me.'

It really was quite bizarre. I would have expected that a child her age who had seen their parent collapse in front of them before being taken to stay with a stranger would be weepy or anxious, or at least a little bit quiet and subdued. Kirsty, however, seemed full of life and entirely unaffected by the day's traumatic events.

'I need to have a quick word with Kate in the kitchen so I'll put the TV on and you can watch a cartoon while we have a chat,' I told her. 'I'll show you your bedroom later.'

'I don't like cartoons,' she scowled.

'Well, you can find something you do like for ten minutes,' I said, handing her the remote.

Kate and I walked through to the kitchen.

'She seems full of energy,' I said, putting Ryan down in his playpen.

'Yes, she certainly is,' sighed Kate.

'I'm afraid I've got to rush off somewhere now,' she added. 'So tell me, what do you need to know?'

She had put me a bit on the spot.

'Oh, er, OK,' I said. 'Is she on any medication and what do I need to do about school?'

It was Thursday so I was assuming that she'd be going the following day.

'She's not on any medication and don't worry about school,' said Kate. 'After everything that's happened, she can have the day off tomorrow. I've already rung the school and told them.

'Coincidentally they've got an inset day on Monday and anyway she'll probably be back home by then.'

By the sounds of it, this was going to be another short respite placement.

'By the way, Kirsty's been with Mike and Pat for so long she calls them Mum and Dad,' she told me.

'That's fine,' I said. 'Have you heard any more about how her mum is?'

'When I leave here I'm going to give Mike a call so I'll let you know if there are any updates,' she said.

'Before I go, shall we quickly take Kirsty up to her bedroom so I can check it?' asked Kate. 'I'm sorry, but you know it's procedure now.'

'Of course,' I said.

Guidance had recently been brought in that said whenever a foster parent took on a new child, the child's social worker had to check where they would be sleeping. This was because there had been reports about a couple of foster carers who, desperate to get more money, had squashed several children into one room with just mattresses on the floor rather than proper beds.

I picked up Ryan and we went to get Kirsty from the front room.

'Maggie's going to show us where you're going to be sleeping,' Kate told her.

'Yippee!' She smiled, jumping up.

We all trooped upstairs to the bedroom and Kirsty looked around.

'This is a lovely room, isn't it, Kirsty?' said Kate. 'I'm sure you'll be very comfy here for the next few days.'

'It's OK,' she huffed. 'But I don't like the pink blanket. Remember, Maggie, I told you I didn't like pink? I'd be OK with a blue one or a red one cos I like red too. Or yellow. Just not pink, cos it makes me feel sick.'

This child certainly liked to talk.

'That's not a problem,' I told her. 'I can get you another blanket.'

'Look at all these beds,' she sighed. 'Which one shall I sleep in? I like the bottom bunk, but I like the top bunk too cos you can see everything from up high, but then I might fall out and hurt myself.'

'Right, well, I'd better be going,' said Kate, interrupting Kirsty's monologue.

'I'll come down with you and see you out then I can bring Kirsty's stuff up,' I said, wanting a few minutes alone with Kate.

'She likes to talk,' I said to Kate as I opened the front door.

'Yes, it's incessant,' she said. 'I think it's when she's anxious or nervous and I suppose it's not surprising after what happened today.'

I really felt for Kirsty.

'Keep me updated if you hear anything from the hospital,' I told her.

'I will,' she said. 'I'll give Kirsty a call tomorrow.'

After Kate had gone, I went back upstairs with the small holdall that she had brought containing Kirsty's pyjamas and a couple of changes of clothes.

I sat down on the bed with Ryan on my knee.

'How are you feeling, Kirsty?' I asked. 'You've had a long day. It must have been so scary for you when your mum collapsed.'

'She'll be OK.' She shrugged. 'Kate said the doctors will make her better.

'Can I have some tea now?' She smiled. 'I'm hungry.'

She didn't quite seem to grasp the seriousness of what had happened. All I could hope was that Kate was right and Kirsty's foster mum was going to pull through, because it was going to be one heck of a shock for this little girl if she didn't.

TINY PRISONERS

Evie and Elliot are scrawny, filthy and wide-eyed with fear when they turn up on foster carer Maggie Hartley's doorstep. They're too afraid to leave the house and any intrusion of the outside world sends them into a panic. It's up to Maggie to unlock the truth of their heart-breaking upbringing, and to help them learn to smile again.

THE LITTLE GHOST GIRL

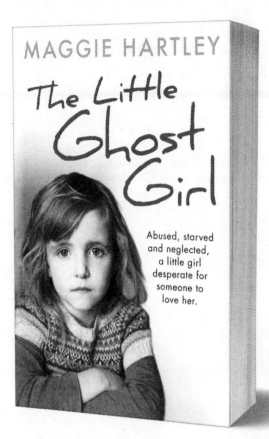

Ruth is a ghost of a girl when she arrives into foster mother Maggie Hartley's care. Pale, frail and withdrawn, it's clear to Maggie that Ruth had seen and experienced things that no 11-year-old should have to. Ruth is in desperate need of help, but can Maggie get through to her and unearth the harrowing secret she carries?

TOO YOUNG TO BE A MUM

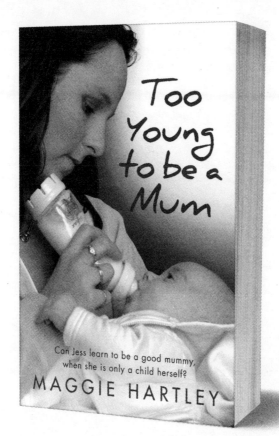

When sixteen-year-old Jess arrives on foster carer Maggie Hartley's doorstep with her newborn son Jimmy, she has nowhere else to go. With social services threatening to take baby Jimmy into care, Jess knows that Maggie is her only chance of keeping her son. Can Maggie help Jess learn to become a mum?

WHO WILL LOVE ME NOW?

When ten-year-old Kirsty arrives at the home of foster carer Maggie Hartley, she is reeling from the rejection of her long-term foster family. She acts out, smashing up Maggie's home. But when she threatens to hurt the baby boy Maggie has fostered since birth, Maggie is placed in an impossible position; one that calls into question her decision to become a foster carer in the first place...

SOLD TO BE A WIFE

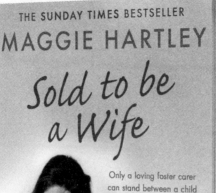

Fourteen-year-old Shazia has been taken into care over a fears that her family are planning to send her to Pakistan for an arranged marriage. But with Shazia denying everything and with social services unable to find any evidence, Shazia is eventually allowed to return home. But when Maggie wakes up a few weeks later in the middle of the night to a call from the terrified Shazia, it looks like her worst fears have been confirmed...

DENIED A MUMMY

THE SUNDAY TIMES BESTSELLER

MAGGIE HARTLEY

Denied a Mummy

The heartbreaking story of three little children searching for someone to love them

Maggie has her work cut out for her when her latest placement arrives on her doorstep; two little boys, aged five and seven and their eight-year-old sister. Having suffered extensive abuse and neglect, Maggie must slowly work through their trauma with love and care. But when a couple is approved to adopt the siblings, alarm bells start to ring. Maggie tries to put her own fears to one side but she can't shake the feeling of dread as she waves goodbye to them. Will these vulnerable children ever find a forever family?

TOO SCARED TO CRY

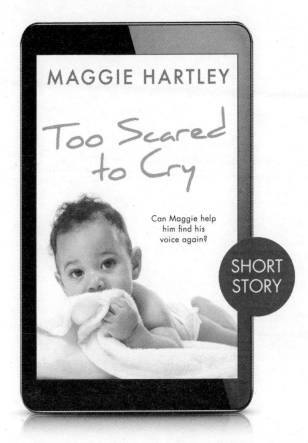

A baby too scared to cry. Two toddlers too scared to speak. This is the dramatic short story of three traumatised siblings, whose lives are transformed by the love of foster carer Maggie Hartley.

A FAMILY FOR CHRISTMAS

A tragic accident leaves the life of toddler Edward
changed forever and his family wracked with guilt.
Will Maggie be able to help this family grieve for the son
they've lost and learn to love the little boy he is now?
And will Edward have a family to go home to
at Christmas?

THE GIRL NO ONE WANTED

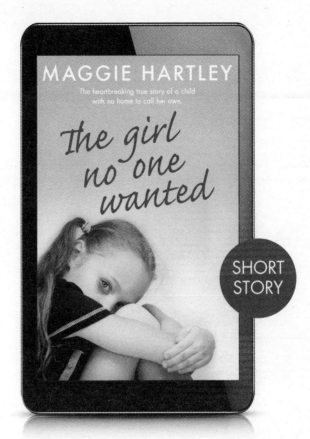

Eleven-year-old Leanne is out of control. With over forty placements in her short life, no local foster carers are willing to take in this angry and damaged little girl. Maggie is Leanne's only hope, and her last chance. If this placement fails, Leanne will have to be put in a secure unit. Where most others would simply walk away, Maggie refuses to give up on the little girl who's never known love.

IS IT MY FAULT MUMMY?

Seven-year-old Paris is trapped in a prison of guilt.
Devastated after the death of her baby brother, Joel,
Maggie faces one of the most heartbreaking cases yet as
she tries to break down the wall of guilt surrounding this
damaged little girl.